HOME ON THE RANGE

HOME ON THE RANGE

by
Deadwood Publishing Ltd.
P.O. Box 564, Station G
Calgary, Alberta
Canada T3A 2G4

First edition September 1982
Second edition January 1983
Third edition September 1984
Fourth edition June 1985

Designed and printed by
Centax of Canada
1048 Fleury Street
Regina, Saskatchewan
Canada S4N 4W8

Photography by:
The Phoebus Communications Group Ltd.
Calgary, Alberta, Canada

Preface . . .

Interest rates are rising. The economy is falling. Unemployment is up. The stock market is down. A loaf of bread costs more but a bushel of grain costs less.

What to do . . . in the face of such unhappy news?

Cook, of course.

For years, housewives have reacted to the ups and downs of life in the only way possible for them — they've headed off to the kitchen to do their best (or worst) there.

So, with all the bad news and bad luck hitting farmers and small businesses everywhere, we decided to take the traditional route through the kitchen . . . and come out in the marketplace with a cookbook.

So we did . . . and here it is.

Home on the Range.

Our cookbook begins with pancakes. That's the only thing that Dad could bake when he began homesteading. Things picked up considerably when our Mom came on the scene with her knack for breads and desserts and thrifty main meals. So we include her thoroughly sensible, down-to-earth recipes, those things that taste like home and youth and more, please!

We include as well some thoroughly modern recipes from the files of the five children that grew up on that farm.

Thus, the cookbook "Home on the Range" is at once a basic, thrifty, sensible cookbook, full of family favorites and country classics.

It's also an extension of the old favorites into some delicious new territories!

In other words, there's something for everyone — old and young, ambitious and un, modern and old fashioned, town and country.

Try us. You'll like what you taste!

HOME ON THE RANGE *was written and published by five members of one family. They include Mrs. John Sorenson of Dixonville, Nancy Millar of Calgary, Margie Sorensen of Dixonville, Karen Burgess of Grande Prairie, Susan Morash of Calgary.*

ALL OF US WANT TO THANK . . .

— our parents, first of all.

— all the other relatives, neighbours and friends who gave us recipes and thus gave of themselves. We remember especially Blanche and Harry Beebe, Mrs. Albert Banks, Dawn Stephenson, Rita Burton, Mrs. Elizabeth Pedersen, Aunt Mable Creighton and Maxine Olson.

— all the other women, our sisters in the kitchen, who developed a new way of cooking food and then passed that method on to others. We were very aware throughout the preparation of our book that very few recipes are entirely new and original. We want to thank those who went before us.

— the Beaverlodge Research Station for pictures on page 12, 30, 156 and 174; the Peace River Centennial Museum for picture on page 84; the Red Deer Centennial Museum for picture on page 144, and most especially Mrs. Jean Fentie of Fairview for the picture of her dad, Oscar Johnson, on page 43. Mr. Johnson took this picture himself to prove to the folks at home that he was managing very nicely as a bachelor on a northern homestead.

— our respective husbands and kids who faithfully ate all the trials and learned to criticize constructively. We hope they'll have the weight off soon!

HOME ON THE RANGE *recipes are given in both standard and metric measurements. We tested all the recipes in their original form, the standard, and then converted them to metric with what's known as the common metric replacement method. This method doesn't produce exact conversions but comes very close. Exact conversions sometimes result in awkward fractions and sizes, so the replacement method rounds up or down for ease in measuring.*

TABLE OF CONTENTS

HOME ON THE RANGE

This is the story of every farm and every family. It's a story told in several dimensions — with anecdotes and old pictures and most of all . . . recipes.

The farm we're concerned with and the family we come from happens to be in the Peace River country of Alberta. But it could have been in the interior of British Columbia or the south of Saskatchewan or anywhere else in western North America where men and women came seeking 160 acres of land . . . to make a start, to make a family, to make a home.

By telling our story, we're telling some of your story too.

In 1923, our Dad came to the United States from Denmark. He brought only youth, ambition, strength and innocence. He had no money and he had no English.

There were four boys in the family. My grandmother Sorensen sent them all to North America because there was no room left in Denmark and no possibilities for the sons of poor tenant farmers.

Three of the brothers stayed. North America never took with Uncle Viggo.

But Dad and Uncle Carl and Uncle Albert were built of sterner stuff. They found work and found friends and managed to survive. In 1928, they headed for Canada — for some of that free land they'd heard about.

By the late 1920's, much of the better homestead land had already been claimed north of the border. So they were advised to go further north, young men, further north.

So they did, and filed on three quarters in the Dixonville area near Peace River. Ten dollars apiece.

It wasn't very good land as it turned out, but they felt like kings right then. Imagine — 160 acres of land each. All theirs! All paid for!

Such riches.

They arrived in the spring and managed to put up a log shack and something of a barn before winter hit . . . which was a lucky thing since winter hits like a ton of bricks in that country!

The three brothers divided up the household chores. Dad was responsible for cooking, Uncle Carl for dishwashing and Uncle Albert for laundry and bread baking.

Housekeeping was casual, to say the least. Mom tells about visiting the bachelor establishment one rainy afternoon while the brothers were in the midst of a spirited card game.

The sod roof was leaking in various spots so they had placed syrup cans and various pots under the worst drips. Whenever one or another pot got too full, the dummy in the card game had to empty it outside.

The drips that leaked onto the floor were ignored because the floor was only dirt, after all.

That shaky leaky existence was the beginning of a farm, and a family and a community . . . and it was just like many other beginnings made in this brave new world.

Quick Breads

A Country Breakfast

From top to bottom:
Pancakes
Mrs. Pedersen's Dundee Buns
Muffins Fit For a Queen
Spoon Bread
Boston Brown Bread
Mrs. Wright's Scones
Spiced Date Muffins
Buttermilk Biscuits

We begin our cookbook with quick breads because that's how most homesteaders began. Very few had yeast or milk or eggs at the very beginning so they resorted to the old standbys . . . bannock and pancakes.

Dad became expert at both.

Even now, he can measure out the right amount of flour with his big old mixing spoon, add just so much baking soda, an egg or two, some buttermilk, and fry up a mess of pancakes that put his kids and their cookbooks to shame.

In the early days, pancakes were eaten morning, noon and night, hot and cold, good or bad. Always, they were washed down with syrup. Good old Rogers Golden Syrup was on every table, and it was generally there in its original 5 or 10 pound can. None of these fancy syrup dispensers or squeeze bottles, thanks just the same. The can was good enough.

In fact, the can itself was highly prized. The smaller ones would be recycled into lunch buckets or grease cans. The larger ones might be used for water pails or slop pails. Everything in those days was used and reused.

Another Dane came to live with the three Sorensen brothers the second winter they were in Canada. Dad taught him to make pancakes too, and therein lies a favorite community story.

When Oluf moved to his own farm the next summer, he relied heavily on pancakes. He'd make a big batch in the morning and leave enough for lunch and maybe even supper, in case nothing better came along. He always lived in the hope of something better.

Anyway, he left his pile of pancakes one morning and went off to continue working in one of his fields.

Agner, an irrepressible tease and the practical joker in the community, happened by and saw Oluf's pancakes.

He couldn't resist the temptation. He sat down and ate the rest of the pancakes, then left without leaving a note or explanation of any kind.

Oluf came home expecting to finish the pancakes and discovered their disappearance instead. He couldn't figure out who or what had played this trick on him, but he rather suspected Dad. Agner, of course, brought up the subject of pancakes whenever he could and made sure the matter couldn't be forgotten.

All of which left Dad wondering why Oluf was mad at him and why Agner talked about pancakes all the time! It was the sort of local joke that sustained the pioneers who had very few forms of entertainment other than their own.

Agner eventually confessed and Dad and Oluf went back to being good neighbors and good friends.

Dad also learned how to make bannock, a product that sounds rather uninteresting compared to what is available today. But it had the advantages of being quick, simple, cheap and long lasting. Since it was pretty dry to begin with, it seldom got moldy.

We've included a recipe for bannock (page 13) but as Dad tells it, you took, flour, baking powder, milk if you had it (otherwise water), a bit of salt and you mixed it all together good. If you had raisins, you threw in a handful. The batter was poured into a frypan generally and baked in the oven or cooked slowly on top of the stove.

When ready, you added butter and . . . you guessed it . . . syrup.

The second summer on the homestead the Sorensen's got themselves some chickens and a cow. Cooking improved considerably what with eggs and milk available. They even started making butter.

As Dad recalls, they took an empty syrup can, filled it half full of cream and then took turns shaking it. When the butter finally formed, one of them would separate the butter from the buttermilk, wash the butter and salt it generously.

Then they would pack it into empty tobacco cans.

Naturally, the butter always tasted like tobacco but it was a sight better than nothing!

In the second generation, it was Jim's wife Margie who best tackled and conquered quick breads — including pancakes. It was the ultimate embarrassment, she says, to have to pull out a cookbook to make pancake batter. So she memorized the following formula: 2 teaspoons of baking powder for every cup of flour, ¼-½ cup shortening, a little sugar, 2 or 3 eggs, and enough milk to make a runny batter.

Then into a hot frypan with lots of lard or oil to make the edges crispy. The result . . . a quick, delicious and dependable meal or snack. Just like the first generation had discovered. Some things don't change.

When Dixonville published its history book in 1975, the editorial committee plucked up its nerve and asked former lieutenant-governor Grant MacEwan to come to the official book launching party.

He not only came for the party but stayed overnight for the breakfast the following day as well. By all accounts, including his own, he had a wonderful time.

When I met him five years later in Calgary, he still raved about Margie's pancakes and the strawberry sauce. You see, he was lucky enough to get some of the precious wild strawberry jam — something the rest of us haven't seen nor tasted for years! It's saved for very important people and very special occasions . . . as it should be!

Anyway, our recipes for quick breads follow . . . starting with the bannock, going on through Grant MacEwan's pancakes, biscuits, scones of every description . . . right up to the most modern loaves and biscuits. Read, Eat and Enjoy!

BANNOCK

4 cups flour	1 L flour
1 tsp. salt	5 mL salt
8 tsp. baking powder	40 mL baking powder
1 tbsp. sugar	15 mL sugar
2 cups cold water, about	500 mL cold water, about

Mix the dry ingredients thoroughly and stir in enough cold water to make a thick batter that when poured out, will level out. Mix rapidly with a spoon until completely smooth. Then pour into a greased frypan or baking dish. Fill about one-half full.

Bake about 45 minutes in a hot oven or cook on top of the stove, turning to get both sides done. Test by sticking a knife into the centre of the bannock. If it comes out clean, the bannock should be done.

If lard or drippings were available, they too were added to bannock.

Bannock was a do-it-yourself project, if ever there was one!

Practical jokes were greatly appreciated in the early days. At one sports day in Dixonville, one of the ladies put the following sign on a stall in the barn:

COME AND SEE THE HORSE WITH THE HEAD WHERE THE TAIL SHOULD BE . . .

To see this wonder of nature, one had to pay 5¢.

Inside the stall, a horse was standing back to front with his tail in the manger, his head out the front.

PANCAKES

⅓ cup whole wheat flour	75 mL whole wheat flour
1 cup white flour	250 mL white flour
1 tsp. sugar	5 mL sugar
3 tsp. baking powder	15 mL baking powder
½ tsp. salt	2 mL salt
¼ cup cornmeal, optional	50 mL cornmeal, optional
½ cup oil or melted margarine	125 mL oil or melted margarine
2 eggs	2 eggs
1½ cups milk	375 mL milk

In a large mixing bowl, combine the whole wheat flour, white flour, sugar, baking powder, salt and cornmeal, if desired. Make a well in the centre of the dry ingredients and add the oil, eggs and milk. Beat well.

Pour approximately ⅓ cup (75 mL) of batter per pancake on a hot slightly greased griddle. When bubbly, turn and bake other side.

Serve hot with butter and favorite maple or fruit syrup.

RAISIN PANCAKES WITH FRUIT TOPPING

2 cups flour	500 mL flour
2 tsp. baking powder	10 mL baking powder
1 tsp. baking soda	5 mL baking soda
½ tsp. salt	2 mL salt
2 tbsp. sugar	30 mL sugar
2 eggs, lightly beaten	2 eggs, lightly beaten
¼ cup vegetable oil	50 mL vegetable oil
1¾ cups buttermilk	425 mL buttermilk
½ cup raisins	125 mL raisins

In a large bowl, mix the flour, baking powder, soda, salt and sugar together. Combine the eggs, vegetable oil and buttermilk together and stir into the flour mixture just until moistened. Add the raisins. Drop by spoonfuls onto hot greased griddle or pan.

For the fruit topping, use your imagination. If you have canned saskatoons, get a jar. Or canned apricots or cherries. Perhaps a package of frozen raspberries or strawberries. Drain the juice from the fruit and put it into a small saucepan. Thicken with cornstarch. Then add the fruit and heat through. Serve with hot pancakes.

To copy the success of pancake houses, add a dollop of whipped cream. The kids will think you have lost your mind but they will love it.

The stories about pancakes in the early days are legion. Here's one from the Henry Osterhouse story in the Nampa history book.

"We had an old airtight heater with four jam tins for legs on which we did our cooking. Neither of us ever cooked a meal in our life so we started with pancakes. We ate them for breakfast and supper for many, many days. Finally, one evening, Jerry said, 'What shall we have for supper?'

I answered, 'How about some more pancakes?'

Jerry answered, 'I'm pulling out. I'd rather die a natural death.'

He left and I never heard from him again."

BUTTERMILK SCONES

2 cups flour	500 mL flour
1 tsp. salt	5 mL salt
2 tbsp. sugar	30 mL sugar
1 tsp. baking powder	5 mL baking powder
¼ cup lard	50 mL lard
1 tsp. baking soda	5 mL baking soda
1 cup buttermilk	250 mL buttermilk

Mix together the flour, salt, sugar, baking powder. Rub in the lard as for pastry until the mixture resembles coarse crumbs.

Mix the baking soda with the buttermilk and add all at once to the dry ingredients. Stir until everything is moistened. Divide the dough into three pieces. Lightly knead each piece on a floured board. Pat into a circle ½" (1 cm) thick. Cut each circle into four.

Heat electric frypan to 300-325°F (150-160°C) and grease lightly. Fry the scones until lightly browned on all sides. Watch carefully — these will burn if the frypan is too hot. It works with a heavy cast iron frypan as well. Just make sure the temperature is very low.

You can also bake these in a hot oven (400°F) (200°C) for about 10-12 minutes, but they are quite different in character from the frypan variety. This was the way people in the old country used to make scones — on a griddle — because they always had a fire but not always an oven available.

In the early days, scones were made in every shape and size, at every occasion. Every woman had her own signature recipe.

The traditional recipe for buttermilk scones (above) came from Mrs. Elizabeth Pedersen of Calgary who got it from her mother who got it from her family in Scotland. Mrs. Pedersen remembers that the scones were baked over an open fire in Scotland but in Canada, her mother adapted the recipe to a griddle or frypan.

Grandma Wright's scones which follow are quite different but just as delicious! They too originated in Scotland but were refined by Mrs. Wright who lives in northern Canada and is known all over the north for her . . . you guessed it . . . . scones!

GRANDMA WRIGHT'S SCONES

4 cups flour	1 L flour
2 tsp. baking powder	10 mL baking powder
1 tsp. baking soda	5 mL baking soda
½ tsp. salt	2 mL salt
½ lb. lard (butter or drippings)	250 g lard (butter or drippings)
2 cups brown sugar	500 mL brown sugar
½ cup natural bran	125 mL natural bran
2 cups oatmeal, not instant	500 mL oatmeal, not instant
1 cup wheat flakes	250 mL wheat flakes
½-1 cup currants or raisins	125-250 mL currants or raisins
3 eggs, well beaten	3 eggs, well beaten
1½-2 cups buttermilk	375-500 mL buttermilk

Combine the flour, baking powder, baking soda and salt. Cut in the lard with a pastry blender or by hand until the mixture resembles coarse crumbs. Blend in the brown sugar. Add the bran, oatmeal, wheat flakes, currants or raisins.

Beat the eggs well and mix well with the buttermilk. Make a well in the dry ingredients and pour the wet ingredients in all at once. Mix until dry ingredients have been moistened and then turn out onto a floured surface. Knead until smooth, for just a few seconds.

Pat out into 1" (2.5 cm) thickness and cut into triangles or desired shape. Place on greased baking sheet and bake at 350°F (180°C) until slightly brown on the bottom, about 15-20 minutes.

CURRANT SCONES

2 cups flour	500 mL flour
⅓ cup sugar	75 mL sugar
4 tsp. baking powder	20 mL baking powder
½ tsp. salt	2 mL salt
⅓ cup lard, butter or margarine	75 mL lard, butter or margarine
½ cup currants	125 mL currants
1 egg, well beaten	1 egg, well beaten
¾ cup milk	175 mL milk

Combine the flour, sugar, baking powder and salt. Rub in the shortening until the mixture resembles coarse crumbs. Add the currants.

Beat egg well and add the milk. Pour all at once into the dry ingredients and mix well until everything has been moistened. The dough should be soft without being sticky.

Divide dough into three portions. On a well floured surface, pat each piece into a circle about ½" (1 cm) thick and cut into four pieces. Repeat for the other two portions. Put pieces onto a greased cookie sheet and bake at 400°F (200°C) until golden brown — about 15 minutes.

JAM BUNS

2 cups flour	500 mL flour
3 tsp. baking powder	15 mL baking powder
2 tbsp. sugar	30 mL sugar
¼ tsp. salt	1 mL salt
1 cup butter or margarine	250 mL butter or margarine
1 egg, beaten	1 egg, beaten
1 tsp. vanilla	5 mL vanilla
½ cup milk	125 mL milk

Mix the dry ingredients and cut in the shortening until the mixture resembles coarse crumbs. Beat the egg and add the milk and vanilla. Add the wet to the dry and mix thoroughly.

On a floured surface, roll out the dough about as thick as pie crust. Cut in 3" (7.5 cm) squares; place a dab of jam on each square and fold the four corners up toward the middle. Pinch the edges together and bake in muffin tins at 350°F (180°C) for 20 minutes. Makes about 28.

Debates were popular pastimes in some communities. One northern community once sponsored a debate entitled . . . "Which would you sooner have, a clean crabby housekeeper or a dirty good natured one?"

After much heated discussion, dirty good natured housekeepers were declared the best.

MRS. HARVIE'S ORANGE BREAD

2 oranges, the rind & juice	2 oranges, the rind & juice
1 cup sugar	250 mL sugar
water & juice to make 1 cup	water and juice to make 250 mL
2 tbsp. lard (or butter or margarine)	25 mL lard (or butter or margarine)
1 egg	1 egg
1 cup sugar	250 mL sugar
2¼ cups flour	550 mL flour
2 tsp. baking powder	10 mL baking powder
½ tsp. salt	2 mL salt
1 cup milk	250 mL milk

Squeeze the oranges and set the juice aside. Grind up the rind of the oranges, and add the sugar. Add water to the orange juice to make 1 cup (250 mL) liquid. Add to the rind and the sugar and boil until the mixture is thick and syrupy, about 10 minutes. Add lard or substitutes.

In another bowl, beat the egg and add the sugar. Mix together the flour, baking powder and salt and add to the egg mixture alternately with the milk. Lastly, add the orange syrup mixture. Pour into a greased loaf pan and let rise in a warm place for 20 minutes.

Bake in 350°F (180°C) oven for about an hour.

BANANA AND DATE LOAF

½ cup chopped dates	125 mL chopped dates
½ tsp. soda	2 mL soda
1 cup boiling water	250 mL boiling water
½ cup butter or margarine	125 mL butter or margarine
1¼ cups sugar	300 mL sugar
2 eggs, beaten	2 eggs, beaten
1 cup banana, mashed	250 mL banana, mashed
2½ cups flour	625 mL flour
2 tsp. baking powder	10 mL baking powder
½ cup walnuts	125 mL walnuts

Put the dates and baking soda into small bowl and pour the boiling water over them. Let cool.

Cream the butter or margarine and sugar; add well beaten eggs. Mash the bananas and add to the creamed mixture. Mix the flour and baking powder. Add to the creamed mixture along with the prepared date mixture and the walnuts.

Pour into greased loaf pan and bake for about 50 minutes in 350°F (180°C) oven.

Date loaf and banana loaf turned up everywhere in the early days . . . at teas and bazaars, in lunch buckets, on the supper table. They were steady old standbys that both tasted good and kept the grocery bills down.

Our updated version is a two-for-one bargain and better than ever: Banana Date Loaf.

Another old favorite was Boston Brown Bread. Mom always doubled the recipe and baked it in large juice cans.

She got the recipe one day while she was in town getting her hair cut. She clipped the recipe out of the hairdresser's magazine and got more use out of that than any haircut.

BOSTON BROWN BREAD

1 cup whole wheat or graham flour	250 mL whole wheat or graham flour
½ cup white flour	125 mL white flour
1 cup cornmeal	250 mL cornmeal
1½ tsp. baking soda	7 mL baking soda
1 tsp. salt	5 mL salt
1¾ cups thick sour milk or buttermilk	425 mL thick sour milk or buttermilk
⅓ cup molasses	75 mL molasses
⅓ cup brown sugar	75 mL brown sugar
⅔ cup raisins	150 mL raisins

Combine the flours, cornmeal, soda and salt. Mix together the buttermilk, the molasses and the sugar and add to the dry ingredients. Stir in the raisins.

If you want fairly dainty portions of this bread, divide the dough into three portions and put into large foodcans — approximately 20 oz. (568 mL) size. If you don't mind larger circles, use cleaned coffee cans. Whatever size you use, cut off the top completely before using and grease well. Cover the cans tightly with foil and place on a rack in a large pot — something like a canner or Dutch oven. Pour boiling water into the pot so that the water reaches approximately half way up the cans.

Cover the canner or Dutch oven and let the steaming continue 2½-3 hours, depending on the size of can used.

When done, turn the bread out of the tins onto a baking sheet and put them into a hot oven just long enough to dry the surface — about 3-4 minutes.

This is awfully good as is — with butter. But it also responds well to creamed cheese, lemon butter, cranberry jelly . . . you get the picture.

HOBO BREAD

1½ cups hot water	375 mL hot water
3¾ cups raisins	925 mL raisins
4 tsp. baking soda	20 mL baking soda
4 tbsp. margarine	50 mL margarine
1 cup white sugar	250 mL white sugar
1½ cups brown sugar	375 mL brown sugar
2 tsp. vanilla	10 mL vanilla
1 tsp. salt	5 mL salt
3 eggs	3 eggs
4 cups flour	1 L flour
½ cup chopped walnuts	125 mL chopped walnuts

In a large bowl, pour the hot water over the raisins. Stir in 4 tsp. (20 mL) baking soda and mix well. Add the margarine, white sugar and brown sugar, vanilla, salt, eggs and flour. Mix well. Fold in the walnuts last.

Grease eight 14 oz. cans (or a size thereabouts) and fill half full with the mixture. Bake at 350°F (180°C) for 45 minutes.

In spite of the name, this is nice sliced and buttered for afternoon tea, or a late evening snack. It is spiffier than it sounds.

NO-NONSENSE BRAN MUFFINS

¼ cup shortening	50 mL shortening
2 tbsp. brown sugar	30 mL brown sugar
1 egg	1 egg
½ tsp. vanilla	2 mL vanilla
½ cup molasses	125 mL molasses
1⅓ cups flour	325 mL flour
1 tsp. baking soda	5 mL baking soda
½ tsp. salt	2 mL salt
1 cup bran	250 mL bran
⅔ cup buttermilk	150 mL buttermilk
¾ cup raisins	175 mL raisins

Cream the shortening and sugar; add the egg and beat well. Blend in the vanilla and molasses. Mix together the flour, baking soda, salt and bran and add alternately to the creamed mixture with the buttermilk. Fold in the raisins.

Grease 12 muffin cups and fill them approximately ⅔ full with batter. Bake in 400°F (200°C) for 15-18 minutes.

REFRIGERATOR BRAN MUFFINS

2 cups boiling water	500 mL boiling water
2 cups 10% all bran cereal*	500 mL 10% all bran cereal*
1 cup butter or margarine	250 mL butter or margarine
3 cups sugar	750 mL sugar
4 eggs	4 eggs
4 cups buttermilk	1 L buttermilk
5 cups flour, some whole wheat	1.25 L flour, some whole wheat
3 tbsp. baking soda	50 mL baking soda
1 tbsp. salt	15 mL salt
4 cups bran flakes cereal	1 L bran cereal
2 cups raisins or chopped dates	500 mL raisins or chopped dates

Pour boiling water over the all bran and let stand until cool.

Cream butter or margarine with sugar and add eggs. Add the cooled bran mixture and the buttermilk. Combine the flour, baking soda, salt, bran flake cereal and raisins or dates. Add to the wet ingredients and stir well.

Place in a container that can be tightly covered, cover and place in fridge for at least 24 hours before using. An ice cream plastic pail works well for this purpose.

To bake, place paper baking cups in a muffin tin and fill ¾ full. Bake in a 400°F (200°C) oven for 12-15 minutes.

Bake only as many muffins as you require and put the batter back into the fridge after using. It keeps up to 3 weeks.

*You can also use natural wheat bran.

SPICED DATE MUFFINS

2 cups flour
3½ tsp. baking powder
½ tsp. salt
½ cup sugar
1 cup chopped dates
1 egg, lightly beaten
1 cup milk
⅓ cup melted butter or margarine
2 tbsp. brown sugar
Dash of cinnamon and nutmeg

500 mL flour
20 mL baking powder
2 mL salt
125 mL sugar
250 mL chopped dates
1 egg, lightly beaten
250 mL milk
75 mL melted butter or margarine
30 mL brown sugar
Dash of cinnamon and nutmeg

In a mixing bowl, combine the flour, baking powder, salt, sugar and dates. Add the egg, butter or margarine and milk all at once to the dry ingredients and stir just until moistened. Spoon into prepared greased muffin tins.

Combine the brown sugar and spices. Sprinkle the raw dough with a bit on each muffin. Bake in a 400°F (200°C) oven for 15-20 minutes.

Bread and milk used to be a favorite snack. Everyone had their own way of preparing it.

One family added brown sugar and a little extra cream. Another family liked their bread and milk with syrup. Some people buttered the bread before adding the milk; others preferred it plain. Some added a bit of fresh or canned fruit.

It was a basic combination with endless variations!

JOHNNY CAKE

¾ cup butter or margarine
1 cup sugar
3 eggs
2 cups flour
1 cup cornmeal
3 tsp. baking powder
¼ tsp. salt
1¼ cups milk
1 tsp. cinnamon

175 mL butter or margarine
250 mL sugar
3 eggs
500 mL flour
250 mL cornmeal
15 mL baking powder
1 mL salt
300 mL milk
5 mL cinnamon

Cream the butter or margarine and sugar. Add the eggs one at a time and beat well. Mix together the flour, cornmeal, baking powder and salt. Add alternately to the creamed mixture with the milk.

Pour into a greased 8" x 8" (2 L) baking pan. Before putting into the oven, sprinkle the cinnamon over the top of the batter. This will all change shape as it bakes but there will be a hint of cinnamon nevertheless.

Bake in 350°F (180°C) oven for 30 minutes. Do not overbake. The beauty of this Johnny Cake is its moistness.

BUTTERMILK BISCUITS

3 cups flour	750 mL flour
2 tbsp. sugar	30 mL sugar
4 tsp. baking powder	20 mL baking powder
1 tsp. salt	5 mL salt
½ cup shortening (lard is good)	125 mL shortening (lard is good)
1 cup buttermilk	250 mL buttermilk

In a large bowl, mix the flour, sugar, baking powder and salt. Cut in the shortening with a pastry blender or by hand until the mixture resembles coarse crumbs. Add the buttermilk. Stir only long enough for the dough to form a ball and leave the sides of the bowl.

Dump onto a floured surface and knead gently about 10 times. Pat in 8" (20 cm) square and cut the big square into nine smaller squares. Place squares on a greased baking sheet, about 1" (2.5 cm) apart, and bake in 450°F (230°C) oven for 12-15 minutes.

IRRESISTIBLE TEA BISCUITS

If supper's a bit light in other departments, these biscuits are a wonderful stretcher. Their special quality must have something to do with the fact that lard is used.

2 cups flour	500 mL flour
½ tsp. baking soda	2 mL baking soda
2 tsp. baking powder	10 mL baking powder
½ cup sugar	125 mL sugar
½ tsp. salt	2 mL salt
½ cup lard	125 mL lard
1 cup buttermilk	250 mL buttermilk
Raisins or currants (optional)	Raisins or currants (optional)

Mix together the flour, baking soda, baking powder, sugar and salt. Cut in the lard until the mixture is crumbly. Add the buttermilk and mix just until the dry ingredients are moistened. Add raisins and currants, if you are using them.

Drop by spoonfuls on a greased baking pan; sprinkle with a bit more sugar and bake in 400°F (200°C) oven for about 15 minutes. Don't let them get too brown — just a nice light brown. Serve warm.

WHOLE WHEAT BISCUITS

3 cups whole wheat flour	750 mL whole wheat flour
6 tsp. baking powder	30 mL baking powder
1½ tsp. salt	7 mL salt
½ cup shortening	125 mL shortening
1½ cups milk	375 mL milk

Combine the flour, baking powder and salt. Cut in the shortening until the mixture resembles fine crumbs. Add milk until the dough is soft and puffy.

Turn onto a floured board and knead gently 20 times.

Roll out about ½" (1 cm) thick; cut into rounds and bake in 400ºF (200ºC) oven for 12-15 minutes.

Note: If using margarine or butter, reduce the salt to 1 tsp. (5 mL).

CRANBERRY LOAF

2 cups flour	500 mL flour
1½ tsp. baking powder	7 mL baking powder
½ tsp. baking soda	2 mL baking soda
½ tsp. salt	2 mL salt
1 cup sugar	250 mL sugar
Grated rind from 1 orange	Grated rind from 1 orange
1¼ cup chopped fresh or frozen cranberries	300 mL chopped fresh or frozen cranberries
1 egg, beaten	1 egg, beaten
¼ cup melted butter or margarine	50 mL melted butter or margarine
Juice from 1 orange plus water to make ¾ cup liquid	Juice from 1 orange plus water to make ¾ cup liquid

Combine flour, baking powder, soda, salt, sugar and orange rind; mix thoroughly. Stir in cranberries. Combine egg, melted butter and orange juice. Add to dry ingredients, stirring just until blended. Pour into greased 9" x 5" (2 L) loaf pan.

Bake in 350ºF (180ºC) oven for 50 to 60 minutes or until toothpick inserted in centre comes out clean. Cool in pan 10 minutes; remove and cool on rack.

Store at least one day before slicing.

MRS. ELIZABETH PEDERSEN'S DUNDEE BUNS

1 cup raisins	250 mL raisins
1 cup water	250 mL water
¼ cup butter or margarine	50 mL butter or margarine
¾ cup sugar	175 mL sugar
1 egg	1 egg
1½ cups flour	375 mL flour
1 tsp. baking soda	5 mL baking soda
1 tsp. cinnamon	5 mL cinnamon
½ tsp. cloves	2 mL cloves
Liquid from the raisins to equal ½ cup	Liquid from the raisins to equal 125 mL

In a small saucepan, cover the raisins with water. Simmer for 20 minutes. Drain the water from the raisins and let cool, reserving liquid for later.

Cream the butter or margarine with the sugar. Add egg and beat well. Combine the flour, baking soda, cinnamon and cloves. Measure the liquid from the raisins and either add to or remove some in order to have ½ cup (125 mL) liquid. To the creamed mixture, add the dry ingredients alternately with the raisin liquid. Finally, add the raisins. Pour batter into well greased and floured muffin tins.

Bake at 375ºF (190ºC) for about 30 minutes or until tester comes out clean. Let cool in the muffin tins for 5-10 minutes and then lift out carefully.

These are rich muffins and easily broken.

BLUEBERRY MUFFINS

2 cups flour	500 mL flour
1/3 cup sugar	75 mL sugar
1 tbsp. baking powder	15 mL baking powder
1 tsp. salt	5 mL salt
1 egg, well beaten	1 egg, well beaten
1 cup milk	250 mL milk
1/4 cup melted butter or margarine	50 mL melted butter or margarine
1 cup fresh or frozen blueberries	250 mL fresh or frozen blueberries
1 tbsp. sugar	15 mL sugar
1 tsp. grated lemon rind	5 mL grated lemon rind

In a large bowl, mix together the flour, sugar, baking powder and salt. In another bowl, mix the egg, milk and butter or margarine. Add the wet ingredients all at once to the dry ingredients and mix just until batter is moistened. Do not overstir. Batter is supposed to be lumpy.

Fold in the blueberries. Spoon into greased medium sized muffin tins. Sprinkle with the additional sugar and lemon rind.

Bake in 400°F (200°C) oven for 20 minutes or until toothpick inserted in the centre comes out clean.

FRUITED OAT MUFFINS

1 cup flour	250 mL flour
2 tsp. baking powder	10 mL baking powder
1/2 tsp. soda	2 mL soda
1/2 tsp. salt	2 mL salt
1 tsp. cinnamon	5 mL cinnamon
1/2 cup raisins	125 mL raisins
1/4 cup mixed peel	50 mL mixed peel
1 cup rolled oats	250 mL rolled oats
1/3 cup softened margarine	75 mL softened margarine
1/2 cup brown sugar	125 mL brown sugar
2 tbsp. molasses	25 mL molasses
1 egg	1 egg
3/4 cup buttermilk or sour milk	175 mL buttermilk or sour milk
1/2 tsp. vanilla	2 mL vanilla

Mix together flour, baking powder, soda, salt and cinnamon. Add raisins and peel and rolled oats. Stir until fruit is coated.

Cream margarine, blend in brown sugar, molasses and egg. Add dry ingredients alternately with milk, ending with flour mixture. Add vanilla. Fill muffin tins 2/3 full. Bake for about 20 minutes in 375°F (190°C) oven.

MUFFINS FIT FOR A QUEEN

¾ cup butter or margarine	175 mL butter or margarine
½ cup sugar	125 mL sugar
2 eggs	2 eggs
1⅔ cups flour	400 mL flour
2½ tsp. baking powder	15 mL baking powder
½ tsp. salt	2 mL salt
1¼ cup milk	300 mL milk
¾ cup wheat germ	175 mL wheat germ
1 cup raisins	250 mL raisins

Cream the butter or margarine and the sugar. Add the eggs and beat until light and fluffy. Mix together the flour, baking powder and salt. Add alternately with milk to the creamed mixture, beginning and ending with a dry installment. Add the wheat germ and raisins.

Thoroughly grease 16 large muffin tins, or a 12 member muffin tin but have some foil tins or small containers of some sort ready to take the overflow. This is really enough for 16 good sized muffins. Fill the prepared muffin tins ⅔ full and bake in 350°F (180°C) oven for 15-20 minutes.

Milk and milk products were very versatile in the early days. For instance, skim milk was often used for waxing floors. It gave linoleum a nice shine.

Also, surplus butter was sometimes used to grease wagon axles, on the logic that it did just as good a job as grease and was half the cost.

SPOON BREAD

4 cups milk	1 L milk
1 cup cornmeal	250 mL cornmeal
1 tsp. salt	5 mL salt
2 tbsp. butter or margarine	25 mL butter or margarine
4 eggs	4 eggs

In the top of double boiler, scald milk over simmering water. Slowly add the cornmeal and salt, beating with a whip or wooden spoon vigorously until cornmeal is completely mixed in. Cook until thick; then cover and let cook another 15 minutes until the cornmeal is completely cooked. Stir in butter or margarine.

Beat eggs. Add a small amount of cornmeal mush to the eggs, then return eggs and all to the cornmeal mixture. Beat well.

Pour into well greased casserole dish and bake about 40 minutes at 425°F (220°C) until top is lightly browned.

Serve hot (instead of potatoes) with ham or pork. Spoon out portions and eat with lots of butter. Terrific stuff.

RAISIN LOAF

2 cups flour	500 mL flour
2 tsp. baking powder	10 mL baking powder
1 cup sugar	250 mL sugar
½ cup butter or margarine	125 mL butter or margarine
2 eggs	2 eggs
1 cup milk	250 mL milk
1 tsp. vanilla	5 mL vanilla
½ cup raisins	125 mL raisins
2 tbsp. flour	30 mL flour

Combine the 2 cups flour, baking powder and sugar. Cut the margarine or butter in until the mixture resembles coarse crumbs.

In another bowl, beat eggs slightly; add milk and vanilla. Add all at once to the dry mixture. Finally, sprinkle 2 tbsp. (30 mL) flour over the raisins and add to the mixture.

Pour batter into a greased and floured loaf pan and bake at 350ºF (180ºC) for about an hour. Test with a toothpick to make sure it is done.

This is a good basic recipe. Add cherries or nuts to the raisin mixture to make a fruit loaf, or use cherries alone to produce a cherry loaf. Or leave fruit out entirely and just add lemon rind and some lemon juice instead of some of the milk and make a lemon loaf.

ZUCCHINI BREAD

2 cups flour	500 mL flour
3 tbsp. cinnamon	50 mL cinnamon
1 tsp. salt	5 mL salt
1 tsp. soda	5 mL soda
1 tsp. baking powder	5 mL baking powder
1 tbsp. cocoa	15 mL cocoa
3 eggs, beaten	3 eggs, beaten
1 cup white sugar	250 mL white sugar
1 cup brown sugar	250 mL brown sugar
1 cup cooking oil	250 mL cooking oil
3 tbsp. vanilla	50 mL vanilla
2 cups grated zucchini (unpeeled)	500 mL grated zucchini (unpeeled)
½ cup raisins	125 mL raisins
½ cup nuts, chopped	125 mL nuts, chopped

Mix flour, cinnamon, salt, baking soda, baking powder and cocoa together. Set aside.

In large bowl, thoroughly beat eggs, sugars, vegetable oil and vanilla. Stir in dry ingredients. Blend in grated zucchini, raisins and nuts.

Pour into two greased and lightly floured loaf pans. Bake in 325ºF (160ºC) oven for 60-70 minutes.

Yeast Breads

Cooking for the Fair

Back row:
Basic sweet rolls in various shapes
Poppy seed Braid
Mom's Orange Twist Buns

Middle area:
Dilled Cottage Cheese Bread
Yeast Doughnuts
Grandma Canning's Cake Dougnuts
Cinnamon Swirl Loaf
Whole Wheat Bread

Front area:
Crusty Rye Rolls
Sauerkraut Rye Bread
Glazed Cheesecake Rolls

When Mom came on the scene in 1935, quick breads in the Sorensen household took a back seat to yeast breads. Mom had a touch with yeast bread and buns that was — and is — hard to beat.

She can tell by the feel, by the shine and the smell, whether the dough is just right or not. She can put a pile of flour in the bottom of a pot, throw in a few eggs, some yeast, some milk and some salt and make the whole mess turn into smooth living breathing bread dough.

Then to add insult to injury, she can take that dough and tie it into knots or braids, or squash it into molds and it does exactly what it's told and comes back for more. It's incredible. It's also delicious.

Actually, I think it was the apprenticeship at the old black cookstove that gave Mom and most other pioneer homemakers their talent with bread. They couldn't be exact about anything — they had to sense when the dough was ready and when the oven was hot. There were no thermometers and dials to help them out. So they'd punch down the dough and read its temperature and mood. Then they'd open the oven door and stick in an arm in order to read it.

After doing that sort of thing for a few years, what started out as a mere skill ended up being an art form . . . the art of making bread. It's an art that hasn't received its due recognition yet but it should. Books about winning the west should devote at least one chapter to bread and all the plucky souls that figured out how to make it in spite of prevailing conditions.

Remember the old nursery rhyme about "Wash on Monday, iron on Tuesday, bake on Friday, etc."? Women really did abide by that ditty in the early days. Any housewife who hung out her wash on a day other than Monday was noticed and remembered.

Friday was Apple Pie day, the day for baking. That was the day the stove reigned supreme. Whichever kid was of the right age had to keep the woodbox full. Mom had to remember to keep putting wood into the ever-demanding heat box. And woe to Dad if he hadn't remembered to chop enough wood the night before.

But while there's no doubt the stove was a dictator, it was a benign dictator at least. In return for eternal service, it gave heat for cooking and baking, of course, and heat for more mundane things like drying mitts and warming hands. It had a way of drawing people into its circle. As soon as Dad came in from doing chores, he'd rub his hands over the stove. If we got thoroughly chilled walking home from school, we could sit in front of the open oven for awhile. Grandma Creighton would put her feet on the oven door and visit with us as we moved about.

If you were near the stove, you were near the action, that's all there was to it.

According to the old nursery rhyme, Saturday was clean the house day and that included cleaning the stove.

First the ashes had to be taken out. You could always tell exactly where they had been dumped by the telltale dribble of ashes across the yard.

Then the stove itself had to be cleaned — the chrome parts with Bon Ami and the black parts with elbow grease.

The final touch would be a swipe of wax paper to give the old beauty a shine and sparkle for the weekend.

There was always unspoken competition among the women in the community to be recognized as a good cook and to turn out the best baked products. Once a year, the competition became much more direct.

That was the occasion of the Exhibition, held in the early years at the Beaton Creek hall and later moved to Manning with the Battle River Fair. That was the one day of the year when the women of the community trotted out their very best efforts in cooking, baking, sewing, preserving and gardening and stacked them up against one another.

In the light of modern attitudes toward competition and possible failure, it was a gutsy thing those women did — to set their efforts against those of their neighbours. I know there was stiff competition but I don't think friendships were severed or communities split asunder. Once the prizes were awarded, the competitors went back to the drawing boards, as it were, to do better "next year".

The Peace River country is "next year" country in more ways than one!

I remember the Beaton Creek exhibitions best — how the doors would close on those all-important judges and we'd be left outside, wondering and waiting.

Occasionally, we'd see a hand hold up a jar of preserves or a head bend to the task of tasting. It was exquisite agony.

Karen remembers the Battle River exhibition better. By that time, Mom pretty well specialized in yeast products. It was one time of the year that we got doughnuts because one of the categories — a selection of yeast breads — required doughnuts. For us, this was a great treat!

She usually entered a wild cranberry pie as well, and it was a perennial winner. Wild cranberries are wonderfully tart and a pie made out of them is quite out of this world. Civilization and roads have pretty well eliminated wild cranberries . . . and the wild cranberry pie. What a pity.

However, there's still bread and all its wonderful variations. Read, eat and enjoy!

BASIC WHITE BREAD

2 tsp. sugar	10 mL sugar
1 cup lukewarm water	250 mL lukewarm water
2 tbsp. active dry yeast	30 mL active dry yeast
2 cups milk, scalded	500 mL milk, scalded
6 tbsp. sugar	75 mL sugar
4 tsp. salt	20 mL salt
1 cup cold water	250 mL cold water
4 tbsp. butter or margarine	50 mL butter or margarine
11 cups flour, approx.	2.75 L flour, approx.

In a small bowl, dissolve the 2 tsp. (10 mL) sugar in the lukewarm water and sprinkle the yeast on top. Let stand 10 minutes. The yeast should froth considerably.

In a saucepan, scald the milk and add the 6 tbsp. (75 mL) sugar and salt. Stir well. When dissolved, add the 1 cup (250 mL) cold water to bring the mixture to lukewarm. Add the butter or margarine.

Measure 10 cups (2.5 L) flour into a large mixing bowl, making a well in the centre. Keep 1 cup (250 mL) of flour aside to use later, if necessary. Stir up the dissolved yeast, add the milk mixture. Stir well and pour combined liquids into the well in the flour. Mix until well absorbed, using a large spoon. Then with the hands, work the dough until sufficiently blended to turn out onto a floured board. Knead on the floured board about 8 minutes or until smooth and elastic. Reserved flour may be added here if the dough remains sticky.

Rinse out the large mixing bowl with hot water so it will be warm when dough is put back into it. Dry and grease lightly. Put dough into bowl, turn once to coat all sides. Cover well and set away from drafts in a warm place. Allow to rise until double in bulk — 1¾-2 hours.

Turn dough out onto lightly floured surface. cut into four equal parts. Shape each piece into a round ball and let rest 10 minutes while greasing four bread pans, or loaf pans. Shape dough into loaves; put into the bread pans and let rise until double.

Bake in 425°F (220°C) oven for 15 minutes, reduce heat and bake for another 35 minutes at 375°F (190°C). Turn out on rack and allow to cool. While still warm, brush the tops with butter, or a bit of milk and sugar mixed together.

In many pioneer homes, the boys had to do the milking while the girls were responsible for the separating . . . and worst of all, washing the separator.

The separator was a big heavy machine that took the milk in at one end, threw it around, and sent it out the other end — separated into milk and cream. That part was easy.

The hard part was washing the beast and keeping track of all the parts, because once everything was washed and sterilized, it had to go back together again, with nothing left over.

OVERNIGHT BUNS

When you are making a batch of plain white bread, save two cups of the dough to make buns.

2 cups dough	500 mL dough
1 cup sugar	250 mL sugar
½ cup shortening	125 mL shortening
1 egg	1 egg
1 cup warm water	250 mL warm water
½ tsp. salt	2 mL salt
½ cup raisins	125 mL raisins
Flour	Flour

Mix first 7 ingredients thoroughly and add enough flour to make a soft dough. Let stand in a bowl 5-6 hours. Then mold into buns. Place on greased baking sheet and let rise overnight and bake in the morning.

When one pioneer family decided to make the big move to the Peace River country, the women agreed on the condition that the family piano come along.

Everything went well until they came to the end of the rail lines and had to travel the rest of the way by horse power. The horses just couldn't handle that piano plus all the other household goods plus muddy narrow trails. So the piano had to go — temporarily.

The men built a platform near the side of the road and installed the piano upon it. They covered it with spruce boughs and canvas to try to keep the elements off it. And then they promised everyone concerned that they'd be back within two weeks to get the old beauty.

It was two years later before they finally had the time and the resources to get back to the piano. But fortunately it had survived its storage quite nicely and went on to be a very important part of social life in the community for years.

A LITTLE EXTRA

Bread dough	Bread dough
1 cup sour cream	250 mL sour cream
1 tsp. soda	5 mL soda
1 cup brown sugar	250 mL brown sugar
1 tsp. cinnamon	5 mL cinnamon

Grease an angel food pan. When your usual recipe for bread dough has risen and is ready to be shaped into loaves, pinch off some small pieces and form into balls about the size of walnuts. Put them in layers in the greased angel food pan and let them rise. When they are light and ready to be baked, pour the sauce over.

To make the sauce, mix together the sour cream, baking soda, brown sugar and cinnamon. Pour over the risen dough balls. Bake at 325ºF (160ºC) for 30-40 minutes or until done. Watch these carefully — they burn easily. Invert and remove from pan immediately.

BASIC SWEET ROLL DOUGH

2 cups flour	500 mL flour
1 tbsp. active dry yeast	15 mL active dry yeast
1 cup milk	250 mL milk
¼ cup sugar	50 mL sugar
¼ cup shortening	50 mL shortening
1 tsp. salt	5 mL salt
2 eggs	2 eggs
1½-2 cups flour	375-500 mL flour

In a large mixing bowl, combine 2 cups (500 mL) flour and 1 tbsp. yeast. Heat 1 cup (250 mL) milk, ¼ cup (50 mL) sugar, ¼ cup (50 mL) shortening, and 1 tsp. (5 mL) salt until warm, stirring to melt shortening. Add to dry mixture; add 2 eggs. Beat at low speed with electric mixer for ½ minute, scraping bowl. Beat 3 minutes at high speed. By hand, stir in 1½ to 2 cups (375-500 mL) flour to make a moderately stiff dough. Knead on lightly floured surface until smooth — 8-10 minutes. Shape into a ball. Place in greased bowl, turning once. Cover; and let rise until double — 45-60 minutes. Punch down and turn out on lightly floured surface. Cover, let rest 10 minutes.

Shape dough into rolls and place on greased baking sheets. Cover and let rise in a warm place until double — about 30-40 minutes.

Bake at 400ºF (200ºC) until done, 10-15 minutes. Remove from pans and cool on rack.

If desired, brush tops with melted butter, or a mixture of cream and sugar. The buns will look even more delicious that way.

CINNAMON ROLLS

Basic sweet roll dough — above	Basic sweet roll dough — above
½ cup butter or margarine	125 mL butter or margarine
⅔ cup brown sugar	150 mL brown sugar
2 tsp. cinnamon	10 mL cinnamon
¾ cup raisins (optional)	175 mL raisins (optional)

Make up a recipe of basic sweet roll dough and let rise until double in size. Then divide the dough into two pieces. Roll each piece into a 12 x 8" (30 x 20 cm) rectangle. Apply the butter or margarine with a rubber spatula, spreading evenly to within ½" (1 cm) of edges.

Combine the sugar and cinnamon and sprinkle evenly over the rectangles. Add the raisins, if desired. Roll up each piece, starting with the long side; seal the seams by pinching together. Slice each roll into 12 pieces and place cut side down on two well greased pans.

Bake at 375ºF (190ºC) for 18-20 minutes or until nicely browned and thoroughly baked. Drizzle thin icing over warm rolls, if desired or brush with butter while still warm.

WHOLE WHEAT BREAD

¾ cup milk	175 mL milk
½ cup brown sugar	125 mL brown sugar
2 tsp. salt	10 mL salt
½ cup shortening	125 mL shortening
1½ cups warm water	375 mL warm water
2 tsp. sugar	10 mL sugar
2 tbsp. yeast	30 mL yeast
4 cups whole wheat flour	1 L whole wheat flour
2 cups all purpose flour	500 mL all purpose flour

Scald milk. Stir in the brown sugar, salt and shortening. Cool the mixture to lukewarm.

Meanwhile, measure into a large bowl, the warm water. Stir in the 2 tsp. (10 mL) sugar and sprinkle the yeast over top. Let stand 10 minutes and then stir.

To the yeast mixture, add the milk mixture. Then add 2 cups (500 mL) whole wheat and 1 cup (250 mL) all purpose flour. Beat well with an electric mixer for several minutes. Then work in the remaining flour by hand. Knead until smooth and elastic. Place in a greased bowl, brush the top with melted shortening. Cover and let rise in a warm place until double in bulk — about 1¼ hours.

Punch down the dough. Turn out onto lightly floured board and divide into two. Then shape into loaves and place in greased loaf pans. Cover and let rise again for about 1 hour. Bake in a 375ºF (190ºC) oven for about 40 minutes.

GRANDMA'S OATMEAL BREAD

2 tbsp. active dry yeast	30 mL active dry yeast
½ cup warm water	125 mL warm water
1¼ cups boiling water	300 mL boiling water
1 cup rolled oats	250 mL rolled oats
½ cup molasses	125 mL molasses
⅓ cup margarine or butter	75 mL margarine or butter
1 tsp. salt	5 mL salt
5-5½ cups flour	1.25-1.375 L flour
2 eggs, beaten	2 eggs, beaten

In a small bowl, soften yeast in the warm water. In a larger bowl, combine the boiling water, rolled oats, molasses, butter or margarine and salt. Cool to lukewarm. Stir in 2 cups (500 mL) flour and beat well. Add the softened yeast and 2 beaten eggs and beat well. Stir in enough of the remaining flour to make a soft dough. Turn out onto a lightly floured surface and knead until smooth and elastic, 8-10 minutes. Shape dough into a ball.

Place in a greased bowl, turning once to grease entire surface. Cover and let rise in a warm place until double in bulk — about 1½ hours.

Grease 2 loaf pans and shape dough into loaves. Cover and let rise in a warm place until double — about 45-60 minutes. Bake at 375ºF (190ºC) until done — about 40 minutes.

CHEESECAKE ROLLS

1 tbsp. active dry yeast	15 mL active dry yeast
¼ cup warm water	50 mL warm water
1 tsp. sugar	5 mL sugar
3½-4½ cups flour	875 mL-1.125 L flour
⅓ cup sugar	75 mL sugar
½ tsp. salt	2 mL salt
½ cup water	125 mL water
½ cup margarine or butter	125 mL margarine or butter
2 eggs	2 eggs
2 tbsp. margarine or butter, melted	25 mL margarine or butter, melted

FILLING:

2 tbsp. sugar	30 mL sugar
1 tbsp. flour	15 mL flour
¼ cup sour cream	50 mL sour cream
1 pkg. (3 oz.) cream cheese	1 pkg. (85 g) cream cheese
1 tbsp. lemon juice	15 mL lemon juice
¼ tsp. vanilla	1 mL vanilla
1 egg white	1 egg white

FROSTING:

1½ cups icing sugar, sifted	375 mL icing sugar, sifted
1 tbsp. margarine or butter	15 mL margarine or butter
3 tbsp. milk	50 mL milk
½ tsp. vanilla	2 mL vanilla

Dissolve yeast in ¼ cup (50 mL) warm water. Add 1 tsp. (5 mL) sugar. Let stand 10 minutes. In large bowl blend 1½ cups (375 mL) flour, ⅓ cup (75 mL) sugar and salt.

In small saucepan heat ½ cup (125 mL) water and ½ cup (125 mL) margarine until very warm. Add warm liquid, yeast mixture and eggs to flour mixture. Blend at low speed until moistened; beat 2 minutes at medium speed. By hand, stir in ½ to 1½ cups (125-375 mL) flour to form a sticky batter. Cover loosely with plastic wrap and cloth towel. Let rise in warm place until light and doubled in size — about 1 hour. Knead in remaining flour until dough is smooth and elastic — about 5-10 minutes.

Divide dough into 16 parts. Shape each into a ball. Place 3" (7 cm) apart on greased cookie sheets. Brush with melted butter. Cover and let rise in warm place until doubled in size — about 1 hour. While dough is rising, prepare filling. In small bowl, blend all filling ingredients at low speed until smooth. Make 1½" (3.5 cm) wide indentation in centre of each ball. Fill with 1 tbsp. (15 mL) filling mixture.

Heat oven to 375°F (190°C). Bake 10-15 minutes or until golden brown. Remove from pans immediately. Cool 15 minutes. Combine frosting ingredients and frost warm rolls. Store in refrigerator.

CRUSTY RYE ROLLS

½ cup warm water	125 mL warm water
1 tsp. sugar	5 mL sugar
2 tbsp. active dry yeast	30 mL active dry yeast
4 cups rye flour	1 L rye flour
3 cups all purpose flour	750 mL all purpose flour
2 eggs	2 eggs
2 cups milk	500 mL milk
½ cup sugar	125 mL sugar
3 tbsp. butter or margarine	50 mL butter or margarine
1 tsp. salt	5 mL salt

In a small bowl, dissolve the 1 tsp. (5 mL) sugar in the warm water and sprinkle yeast on top. Let stand 10 minutes.

In a large bowl, combine rye flour and all purpose flour. Make a well in the centre and break the eggs into the hole. Using an electric mixer, mix the eggs into the flour around them. Don't try to mix them into all the flour, just into the flour immediately adjacent to the eggs.

Heat milk, sugar, butter or margarine and salt until lukewarm. Add to the eggs and dry mixture. Beat a slightly larger area at low speed ½ minute. Then stir the yeast mixture and add it to the flour mixture. Beat the wet ingredients into the flour in ever increasing circles. Now get your hands into the mixture and work the remaining flour from the sides of the bowl into the centre, kneading until all the flour is worked into the dough. Knead on a floured surface about 10 minutes.

Shape into a ball. Place in a greased bowl, turning once to grease all sides and let rise, covered, until double in size — about 1½ hours. Punch down. Shape into 24 small rolls and place on greased baking sheets. Cover and let rise again until double — about 1 hour.

Bake in 350ºF (180ºC) oven 15-20 minutes or until done.

The first thing a farm wife had to do in the early days was master the art of bread making. It was a "trying" period sometimes but generally homemakers learned to make very good bread and do 40 other things at the same time.

Problems arose during the winter when, according to some of the legends, the bread just wouldn't rise because the house was too cold. It was especially tough for overnight bread and buns. So it was necessary sometimes for the women to take the bread dough to bed with them. I don't know how they managed that messy process, but history books do record that measure!

Most communities eventually got a small flour mill in the vicinity. Harry Smith from Chinook Valley was known as a haywire genius — he could build sawmills and fix engines and even figure out ways to grind wheat into flour. But the product his machine made was pretty heavy, by all accounts. Welcome — but heavy.

If at all possible, people preferred to buy their flour-partly because it was lighter and whiter than home ground flour but also because bought flour came in flour sacks.

Now, flour sacks built the west or at least provided a lot of the underpinning. They were used for diapers, tea towels, tablecloths, sheets, bandages, underwear, even women's dresses.

The label lettering on the flour sacks was difficult to remove and everyone had a different formula for the process. Sometimes the formulas worked and sometimes they didn't.

When they didn't, wonderful community stories resulted.

Like the story about the lady who came out to a dance in a beautifully embroidered dress in front, with the words "Best in the West" faintly showing through on the back.

Or the lady who wore a dress that said, out back, "98 pounds when fully packed!"

When bread making was conquered, homemakers turned their attention to tougher talents — like doughnuts. Mrs. T. Novotny was always well known in our community for her yeast doughnuts. We've included her recipe next. Margie's Mom and grandmother were acknowledged masters of the cake doughnut. That's next after next.

YEAST DOUGHNUTS

½ cup warm water	125 mL warm water
2 tsp. sugar	10 mL sugar
2 tbsp. active dry yeast	30 mL active dry yeast
1 cup milk, scalded	250 mL milk, scalded
½ cup butter or margarine	125 mL butter or margarine
½ cup sugar	125 mL sugar
1 tsp. salt	5 mL salt
6 cups flour	1.5 L flour
6 eggs, well beaten	6 eggs, well beaten
1 tsp. almond flavouring	5 mL almond flavouring
2 lbs. lard or vegetable oil	1 kg lard or vegetable oil

Put the warm water into a small bowl. Add the sugar and dissolve it well. Sprinkle the yeast on top and let stand for 10 minutes.

Scald the milk and add butter or margarine, sugar and salt. Remove to a large bowl and cool to lukewarm. Stir up the yeast mixture, and add to the milk mixture. Add half the flour and beat well.

Beat the eggs well and mix in thoroughly. Stir in almond flavouring. Finally, stir in the remaining flour to make a nice soft dough. Knead lightly for a few minutes.

Place dough in a greased bowl, turn once to cover all sides. Cover and let rise until double in bulk — about 1 hour. Punch dough down.

Roll out to ½" (1 cm) thickness and cut with a doughnut cutter. Heat oil or lard in a deep fat fry pan or heavy pot until 375°F (190°C). Test by dropping the centre of a doughnut into the hot fat. It should brown and rise within a minute if the fat is hot enough.

Slide the doughnuts, a few at a time, into the hot fat. Turn as soon as the bottom browns and the doughnut rises.

Drain on paper towelling. Drizzle with thin icing or sprinkle with sugar.

These freeze well and taste like freshly made doughnuts if you just reheat slightly when serving.

GRANDMA CANNING'S CAKE DOUGHNUTS

1 cup sugar	250 mL sugar
3 tbsp. lard*	50 mL lard*
3 eggs	3 eggs
1 tsp. baking soda	5 mL baking soda
1 cup sour milk or buttermilk	250 mL sour milk or buttermilk
3¼ cups flour	800 mL flour
Pinch of salt	Pinch of salt
½ tsp. nutmeg or cinnamon	2 mL nutmeg or cinnamon
2 lbs. lard or vegetable oil	1 kg lard or vegetable oil

Cream the sugar, 3 tbsp. (50 mL) lard and eggs. Beat well. Dissolve the baking soda in the sour milk or buttermilk. Combine the flour, salt and spice. Add the dry ingredients to the creamed mixture alternately with the milk. The dough should be soft but not sticky. Cover and let rest for 10 minutes.

Roll dough out on a slightly floured board to ½" (1 cm) thickness. Dip doughnut cutter into flour and cut out the doughnuts.

Heat the lard or oil in heavy pot or deep fat fryer to 375ºF (190ºC). Test the temperature by putting in a doughnut centre. If it browns and rises within a minute, then the fat is hot enough. (Or use a thermometer to be precise.)

Slide the doughnuts into the hot fat, a few at a time so there is plenty of room for them to bubble and rise. Turn as soon as the bottom side gets brown. Total cooking time should be about 2-4 minutes. Drain on towelling and roll in sugar.

*Lard was always used in the early days. You can substitute margarine.

CINNAMON SWIRL LOAF

7-7½ cups flour	1.75-1.8 L flour
2 tbsp. active dry yeast	30 mL active dry yeast
2 cups milk	500 mL milk
½ cup sugar	125 mL sugar
½ cup butter or margarine	125 mL butter or margarine
2 tsp. salt	10 mL salt
2 eggs	2 eggs
½ cup sugar	125 mL sugar
2 tsp. cinnamon	10 mL cinnamon

In a large mixing bowl, combine 3½ cups (875 mL) of the flour with the dry yeast.

In a small saucepan, heat the milk, ½ cup (125 mL) sugar, butter or margarine and salt just until the mixture is warm. Stir constantly to melt the shortening. Add to the dry ingredients in the mixer bowl. Add eggs. Beat at low speed with electric mixer for ½ minute, scraping sides of the bowl continually. Beat for another 3 minutes at high speed.

By hand, stir in enough of the remaining flour to make a soft dough. Turn out onto lightly floured surface and knead until smooth and elastic — 5-8 minutes. Shape into a ball. Place in lightly greased bowl, turning once to grease all surfaces.

Cover and let rise in a warm place until double, about 1 hour. Punch dough down. Turn out on lightly floured surface. Divide in half. Cover and let rest 10 minutes. Roll each half into 15 x 7" (40 x 17 cm) rectangle.

Combine the ½ cup (125 mL) sugar and cinnamon. Spread each rectangle with half the sugar-cinnamon mixture. Roll dough up as for jelly roll, beginning with the 7" (17 cm) side. Seal long edge and ends.

Place sealed edge down in two greased loaf pans. Cover and let rise in warm place until almost double — 35-45 minutes. Bake in 375°F (190°C) oven for 35-40 minutes or until done.

Remove from pans and cool on wire rack. Drizzle with light icing, if desired. Good as is, and also good toasted.

AIR BUNS

½ cup warm water	125 mL warm water
1 tsp. sugar	5 mL sugar
1 tbsp. active dry yeast	15 mL active dry yeast
3½ cups lukewarm water	875 mL lukewarm water
½ cup sugar	125 mL sugar
½ cup lard or shortening	125 mL lard or shortening
1 tsp. salt	5 mL salt
1 tbsp. vinegar	15 mL vinegar
9-10 cups flour	2.25-2.5 L flour

In a small bowl, mix the warm water and sugar; then sprinkle the yeast on top. Let rise 10 minutes in warm spot.

In a large bowl, put the lukewarm water, ½ cup (125 mL) sugar, shortening and salt. Add to this mixture the yeast and vinegar. Put flour in, one cup (250 mL) at a time, mixing well after each addition. Use just enough flour so dough will not stick to the hands. Knead sturdily.

In a greased pan, let the bread dough rise in warm place for 2 hours. This warm place is essential. The top of the fridge works in some houses. Whatever you do, get a warm (but not hot) place for the bread to rise.

After 2 hours, punch down and let rise for another hour. Then form into buns and place on greased cookie sheet or pan. Do not put too close together as they rise a good deal. Let rise, covered with a clean cloth, for three hours or until they threaten to walk off the cupboard.

Bake at 375°F (190°C) for 20-25 minutes or until buns sound hollow when lightly tapped.

DILLED COTTAGE CHEESE BREAD

1 tsp. sugar	5 mL sugar
½ cup warm water	125 mL warm water
1 tbsp. yeast	15 mL yeast
1 egg	1 egg
2 tbsp. sugar	30 mL sugar
1 tbsp. soft butter or margarine	15 mL soft butter or margarine
1 tsp. salt	5 mL salt
1 tsp. dill weed	5 mL dill weed
1 tsp. dill seed	5 mL dill seed
¼ tsp. baking soda	1 mL baking soda
1 cup creamed cottage cheese, room temp.	250 mL creamed cottage cheese, room temp.
2½-3 cups flour	625-750 mL flour

In large bowl, dissolve the 1 tsp. (5 mL) sugar in the ½ cup (125 mL) warm water. Sprinkle the yeast over the water and let stand 10 minutes.

Add the egg, 2 tbsp. (30 mL) sugar, butter or margarine, salt, dill weed, dill seed, baking soda and warm cottage cheese. Mix until blended. Add 1 cup (250 mL) flour and mix again until well blended. Gradually work in the remaining flour to make a sticky dough. Cover and let rise in a warm place until double in size — about 1 hour.

Grease a large casserole dish. Punch down the dough and put it into the greased dish. Let rise again about 45 minutes. Bake in a 350ºF (180ºC) oven for 40-45 minutes or until loaf sounds hollow when tapped. While still hot, remove the loaf from pan and cool on a rack. Brush the top lightly with butter to finish it off.

SAUERKRAUT RYE BREAD

3 cups flour	750 mL flour
2 tbsp. cocoa	30 mL cocoa
3 tsp. caraway seed	15 mL caraway seed
2 tsp. salt	10 mL salt
2 tbsp. yeast	30 mL yeast
1 can (12 oz.) beer	1 can (356 mL) beer
¾ cup milk	175 mL milk
⅓ cup molasses	75 mL molasses
¼ cup oil or shortening	50 mL oil or shortening
1 egg	1 egg
1 cup sauerkraut, drained	250 mL sauerkraut, drained
3 cups rye flour	750 mL rye flour
1 cup white flour	250 mL white flour

In a large bowl, combine 3 cups (750 mL) flour, cocoa, caraway seeds, salt and yeast. Blend well.

In a small saucepan, heat the beer, milk, molasses and oil until very warm. (Use candy thermometer, if possible. It should read 120-130ºF. It should not be hot enough to to kill the yeast but just warm enough to get the yeast working). Add the warm liquid and the egg to the dry ingredients. Blend with mixer for three minutes. By hand, stir in the sauerkraut and the rye flour. Mix to form a stiff dough. On a floured surface, knead in as much of the 1 cup (250 mL) white flour as necessary to form a stiff elastic, smooth dough. Knead for about 10 minutes.

Place dough in a greased bowl; cover with a clean tea towel or plastic wrap and let rise in a warm place until light and doubled in size. If you don't have a sunny window, try the top of the fridge. If that is not warm enough, set the oven on warm and let the bread rise there.

Punch down dough and divide in half. Shape into balls and put on a greased cookie sheet. This will produce wide flat loaves. If you prefer tall, neat loaves, put the dough into two loaf pans. Cover and let rise until double — about 45-60 minutes.

Bake about ½ hour at 350ºF (180ºC). Loaves should sound hollow when tapped with a finger or knife handle. Remove from pans immediately.

COTTAGE CHEESE ROLLS

⅔ cup walnuts, finely chopped	150 mL walnuts, finely chopped
⅔ cup brown sugar	150 mL brown sugar
3 tbsp. butter, softened	50 mL butter, softened
1 tsp. vanilla	5 mL vanilla
2 tsp. sugar	10 mL sugar
½ cup warm water	125 mL warm water
2 tbsp. yeast	30 mL yeast
3 cups flour	750 mL flour
½ tsp. salt	2 mL salt
¼ cup sugar	50 mL sugar
1 cup creamed cottage cheese*	250 mL creamed cottage cheese*
½ cup butter or margarine, melted	125 mL butter or margarine, melted
1 egg	1 egg

Mix together the first 4 ingredients and save for filling. Dissolve 2 tsp. (10 mL) sugar in lukewarm water and sprinkle yeast over. Let stand 10 minutes.

In a large bowl, combine flour, salt and ¼ cup (50 mL) sugar. Make a well and add the cottage cheese, the melted butter, the yeast mixture which should be stirred up first, and the egg. Mix well. The dough should be sticky. Turn out and knead several times to coat with flour.

Roll into a 12" (30 cm) square. Spread with the prepared filling and roll up. Cut crosswise into 18 slices. Place on greased baking sheets. Cover and let rise for about 1 hour. Bake at 375ºF (190ºC) for 20-25 minutes.

*The cottage cheese should be at room temperature.

No Knead Hot Cross Buns

½ cup milk	125 mL milk
¼ cup shortening	50 mL shortening
1 tbsp. sugar	15 mL sugar
1 tsp. salt	5 mL salt
1 tbsp. yeast	15 mL yeast
½ cup warm water	125 mL warm water
1 tsp. sugar	5 mL sugar
1 egg	1 egg
½ cup raisins or currants	125 mL raisins or currants
½ tsp. cinnamon	2 mL cinnamon
4 cups flour	1 L flour
1 egg white	1 egg white
2 tbsp. cold water	25 mL cold water

Scald milk and add the shortening, 1 tbsp. (15 mL) sugar and salt. Cool to lukewarm.

In the meantime, add the 1 tsp. (5 mL) sugar to the ½ cup (125 mL) warm water and sprinkle yeast over. Let stand 10 minutes. Stir.

Add the yeast mixture to the cooled milk mixture. Blend in the egg, raisins and cinnamon. Gradually work in the flour. Cover and let stand 15 minutes.

Shape dough into 15 buns. Place on greased baking sheet. Let rise in warm place until double in size. Beat the egg white and water until frothy. Brush over tops of buns. Cut cross in top of each bun with scissors.

Bake in 375ºF (190ºC) oven 15-20 minutes. If desired, fill in the crosses with icing made of icing sugar and cream. Best when fresh out of the oven.

Mom's Orange Twist Buns

1 tsp. sugar	5 mL sugar
¼ cup warm water	50 mL warm water
1 tbsp. dry yeast	15 mL dry yeast
½ cup orange juice	125 mL orange juice
¼ cup sugar	50 mL sugar
1 tsp. salt	5 mL salt
¼ cup melted shortening	50 mL melted shortening
3 cups flour	750 mL flour
1 egg	1 egg
1 tbsp. grated orange rind	15 mL grated orange rind
2 tbsp. melted butter or margarine	25 mL melted butter or margarine

ORANGE SUGAR:

¼ cup sugar	50 mL sugar
1 tbsp. grated orange rind	15 mL grated orange rind

In a small bowl, dissolve the 1 tsp. (5 mL) sugar in the ¼ cup (50 mL) warm water. Sprinkle the yeast over the mixture and let stand 10 minutes.

Heat the orange juice to lukewarm. Add the sugar, salt, shortening and 1 cup flour (250 mL). Beat well. Add the softened yeast, egg and orange rind. Add enough additional flour (about 2 cups) (500 mL) to make a soft dough. Knead on lightly floured surface until smooth and satiny.

Place in greased bowl and lightly grease the top. Cover and let rise in a warm place until double in bulk — about 2 hours. Punch down. Let rise 10 minutes.

Roll into a rectangle 12 x 18" (30 x 45 cm). Brush with melted butter or margarine and sprinkle with orange sugar. Fold over in thirds to form a rectangle 12 x 6" (30 x 15 cm). With a sharp knife, cut into strips ¾" (2 cm) wide by 6" (15 cm) long. Grasp the ends of each strip, roll in the opposite directions and then bring ends together to form a circle. Seal ends and place on a greased baking sheet. Let rise about 45 minutes. Bake in a 350ºF (180ºC) oven 15-20 minutes. Yields 16 orange twists.

You can use any basic sweet dough recipe to make these buns. Substitute some orange juice for some of the liquid.

SESAME OR POPPYSEED BRAIDS

2 tsp. sugar	10 mL sugar
2 cups warm water	500 mL warm water
2 tbsp. active dry yeast	30 mL active dry yeast
¼ cup honey or sugar	50 mL honey or sugar
¼ cup oil or soft butter	50 mL oil or soft butter
1 tsp. salt	5 mL salt
2 eggs plus 1 egg yolk, beaten	2 eggs plus 1 egg yolk, beaten
2 cups whole wheat flour	500 mL whole wheat flour
4 cups all purpose flour*	1 L all purpose flour*
1 egg white	1 egg white
1 tbsp. water	15 mL water
sesame seeds or poppyseeds	sesame seeds or poppyseeds

In a large mixing bowl, dissolve sugar in the warm water. Sprinkle in yeast and let stand 10 minutes. Add honey, oil or butter, salt, beaten eggs, whole wheat flour and 1 cup (250 mL) all purpose flour. Beat 2 minutes with electric mixer or vigorously by hand. Gradually work in remaining flour.

Knead on floured board until soft and springy, about 8 minutes. Place in greased bowl, turning to grease dough all over. Cover and let rise about 1 hour. Punch down.

Divide dough into 6 equal parts. Shape each into a long rope about 14" (35 cm) long. Place 3 ropes side by side on greased baking sheet.

Sprinkle each strip with sesame seeds or poppyseeds. Then braid together loosely, tucking in the ends and pinching ends to seal. Repeat with remaining 3 pieces on another greased baking sheet.

Beat egg white lightly with water. Brush tops of loaves with the egg white mixture and sprinkle with more sesame seeds or poppyseeds. Let rise about 45 minutes.

Bake in 375°F (190°C) oven for about 35 minutes or until loaves sound hollow when tapped. Cool on racks.

*You may also use 3½ cups (875 mL) all purpose flour with ½ cup (125 mL) wheat germ.

One lady swears on a stack of Bibles that she buried a bad batch of bread one day so that her husband wouldn't find out about it. The trouble was the bread kept rising whenever the sun hit it for the next few days and she had to keep heaping on more dirt.

Then there's the story of the greenhorn cook who decided to tackle a steamed pudding for Christmas dinner. The instructions in the cookbook said to suspend the pudding over boiling water.

So . . . the lady in question hammered a spike into the beam above their Quebec heater. She tied the pudding into a bag, attached it to a long cord and dutifully suspended it over boiling water . . . about two feet over the pot of water boiling on the heater.

The pudding would be cooking still if a neighbour hadn't happened along to give more precise instructions.

Main Meals

Sunday Dinner

From front to back:
    Pork Roast with Vegetables
    Cornish Game Hens, I Dare You
    Curried Orange Rice
    Vegetable Garden Pie

When Dad and Uncle Carl went out to survey their new land, they came across an animal unfamiliar to them.

"It must be a mule," Carl said. "It has big ears."

They carried on with their work expecting the mule to take off at any time. After all, why would a mule mind what they were doing?

Dad moved closer until he was only about 30 feet away from said mule. Carl was some 90 feet back at the end of the 66 foot surveying wire. He was still assuring Dad that the "mule" was perfectly tame.

Suddenly, the animal began to paw the ground and look downright menacing. Dad and Carl realized they'd better do something quickly — but what? There were no trees big enough to climb and no fences to jump. It was just them, an angry animal and lots of open space.

They did the only thing they could under the circumstances . . . they stood very still and hoped for the best.

After a few minutes, the moose trotted off with two newly born calves in tow. Dad and Carl, those two innocents from abroad, had stumbled onto a cow moose with new babies, a formidable foe at the best of times.

That was their introduction to the moose, an animal that was to grace our dinner table a great deal in the next 40 years.

In the early days, it wasn't too tough to shoot a moose. They came right up to the strawstacks and granaries. In later years, as more and more land was cleared and fenced, hunting expeditions had to go further afield. But most households routinely got a moose in the fall.

Before freezers, the carcass would be kept in a barrel or box outside in the winter months. Or, it would be cut up and canned.

Mrs. Albert Banks instructed Dad in the art of canning moosemeat. "Just put the meat in jars, seal them good and boil the jars in hot water for three hours," she said.

So they did, and lived to tell the tale.

Canned moosemeat was really very good. The meat was thoroughly tenderized in the processing and when combined with various vegetables made wonderful stews.

Because potatoes were a part of every meal — except breakfast — gravy was always vital to help wash down the potatoes. Canned moosemeat made wonderful gravy.

So did fresh or frozen moosemeat for that matter. If it was stewed or steamed for a suitable time, it lost some of its gaminess and was quite tender, and very tasty.

So moose meant a lot to us in those early days.

So did beans. Dad learned how to cook white navy beans from Mrs. Harbke and he kept a pot going most of the time after that. Mom came along and refined the art by adding molasses, tomatoes, onions, brown sugar and whatever else fit her fancy. They became a staple in our household.

We also had the pick of wild birds — partridges, prairie chickens, ducks and wild geese. In fact, Dixonville became well known as a goose hunters' paradise and on that reputation lies several community tales.

The local schoolteachers, Bill and Babe McGrath, decided to join some Edmonton hunters one fall in a hunt on Dad's big field. They all came out the previous evening to dig the pits and arrange the cover and decoys. Geese always came over at the crack of dawn so all these arrangements had to be made the night before.

Then, just for a lark, the McGraths decided to spend the night in a nearby straw stack. Mom remembers Mrs. McGrath saying, "Imagine being 27 years old and never having slept in a straw stack." So they did.

In the early morning, the men went to the prepared pits and Mrs. McGrath was told to stay still and hidden in the strawstack. All went well until the geese started coming in and Mrs. McGrath couldn't see from her straw pile. So she stood up to get a better view and of course the geese saw her, veered away and prevented the hunt. She didn't live that down for a long time.

There wasn't a lot of fussing over main meals in the early days. Homemakers cooked whatever they had. Meat or fowl was generally baked or stewed. Potatoes were boiled. Vegetables were cooked and presented as is. There weren't casseroles or seven layer dinners or seven course meals. That all came later. Whatever fussing that was done was done with the breads or desserts. Main meals were seen as a straightforward presentation of whatever was available.

The same thing held true for community occasions. Chicken suppers were wonderful. Fresh chickens would be fried and then gravy made from the drippings, complete with all the crispy bits left from the frying process. Along with the chicken, there would be mashed potatoes, mashed turnips, creamed peas and carrots — if the gardens had been generous — and coleslaw — if they hadn't.

The menu didn't change substantially over the years. It remained a matter of fresh food cooked as well as possible and presented in a no-nonsense way.

There's a moral, I think, in that story.

The biggest test of a farm wife was the threshing crew. Before most farms got their own threshing machines or combines, threshing crews used to go from farm to farm, threshing the grain at one farm and then moving on to the next.

The crews would be anywhere from 6-12 men, and they had to be fed three big meals a day and one afternoon lunch.

Nobody got out of work when the threshers were there. Little kids had to fill the woodbox continuously and stay out of trouble. Bigger kids had to help outside with the horses and machinery or inside with the cooking. Grandmas had to give up their peace and quiet and join forces for a few days. It was a real ordeal and if a homemaker managed to serve good meals, on time, in good humour, then her reputation was made.

Breakfast had to be bacon and eggs and porridge or pancakes. Dinner, the midday meal, had to be meat and potatoes and bread and dessert. Ditto for supper. In between, there had to be sandwiches and a sweet, plus gallons of coffee, tea and juice.

There wasn't time to be fancy. A roast went in the oven right after breakfast and a ham would go in right after dinner. Pots of gravy had to be made to wash down the potatoes. Vegetables were OK as long as there were lots of other things. And dessert was expected to be generous.

As a kid, I remember peeling mostly. I'd peel potatoes and then I'd peel carrots and then turnips. It went on and on . . . not to mention dishes!

We have some thresher type recipes in the cookbook, but not very many. Nowadays, big meals are out and small is beautiful. The recipes from the second generation reflect that trend. But it's fun to remember.

It's also fun to remember the simplest, most straightforward meal of all enjoyed by the bachelors way back then.

Dad tells me that sometimes when the three brothers came in from work, he would start the fire, fill the kettle and put it on to boil.

In the meantime, Albert would gather the eggs and put six into a little sugar sack. After tying the sack shut, he'd put it into the water gradually heating in the kettle. Once the kettle boiled and the eggs were done, he'd take them out of their sack and put them on the table.

At that point, Dad would make tea with the remaining water.

Carl would already have cut the bannock and opened the syrup.

And so . . . . supper was served.

We offer you that suggestion along with many others in the following sections. Read, eat and enjoy!

CANNED MOOSEMEAT

First of all, bag a moose.

After the meat is adequately chilled and cleaned, cut it across the grain 1" thick (2.5 cm) in jar length pieces, or cut in cubes as for stew. Trim excess fat and gristle. Pack the meat into the jars raw or lightly brown first.

To each jar, add ½ tsp. (2 mL) salt and a sprinkle of pepper. Partially seal the jars with rubber rings and zinc caps by screwing caps down firmly and then turning the caps back ¼" or ½ cm. Process immediately for 3 hours.

Have the water in the processing kettle or canner hot, but not boiling. Lower jars into the canner slowly and be sure they don't touch. Also, be sure there's a rack or board on the bottom of the boiler or canner. Cover the jars with water and begin timing when the water comes to a rolling boil.

Throughout the process, keep the water boiling gently; if it gets too energetic, some of the liquid that builds up in the jars may leak out. Add more water during the processing stage, if necessary.

After processing, lift the jars from the water and place on a thick cloth or board to cool. Do not tighten self-sealing caps but, if using the rubber rings and zinc caps, seal them as soon as you remove them from the processing vessel. Screw the lids down tight.

Cool the jars upright with space between each one. Avoid drafts.

Housewives were very glad when freezers were invented. The canning process — especially of meats — was always fraught with anxiety. If canned fruits spoiled, they tended to ferment which wasn't entirely unwelcome. But if canned meats or vegetables weren't sealed just right, the product could have been deadly.

That's why the community "locker" became so popular. Butcher shops supplied cold storage lockers, for a fee, and farmers stored their game or beef or pork that way.

Every time Dad went "into town", he was instructed to pick up some meat from the locker. He would do so and then Mom would cook whatever turned up.

STUFFED MOOSE STEAK OR MOCK DUCK

¼ cup flour	50 mL flour
salt and pepper	salt and pepper
1½ lbs. moose steak	750 g moose steak
½ cup butter	125 mL butter
¾ cup chopped onion	175 mL chopped onion
¾ cup chopped celery	175 mL chopped celery
3 cups dry bread crumbs	750 mL dry bread crumbs
salt and pepper to taste	salt and pepper to taste
4 slices bacon	4 slices bacon
1 cup water or tomato juice	250 mL water or tomato juice

Carefully remove any fat from the meat as it is the fat of wild animals that gives it a gamy flavour. Mix the ¼ cup (50 mL) flour with salt and pepper. Dip the steak into the flour and pound the flour in with a mallet or blunt edge of a plate.

Melt the butter in a fry pan. Saute the onion and celery for about five minutes, until the onion is transparent and the celery slightly browned. Add the bread crumbs and salt and pepper.

Spread the dressing on the steak. Roll it up, wrap with string, and tie. Place in a roaster pan and arrange the bacon slices over the steak. Add one cup (250 mL) water or tomato juice.

Bake in a 325ºF (160ºC) oven until tender, about 3 hours. Keep roaster lid on. Baste frequently and see that the moisture doesn't entirely evaporate. Add more, if necessary. Moose tends to be dry and needs to be braised frequently.

Also try this with some of the cheaper cuts of beef steak. The combination is then known as mock duck.

ROAST WILD GOOSE

1 wild goose	1 wild goose
juice of 1 lemon	juice of 1 lemon
6 cups stuffing	1.5 L stuffing
2 tbsp. butter	25 mL butter
salt & pepper to taste	salt & pepper to taste
2 cups water, or	500 mL water, or
2 cups fruit juice	500 mL fruit juice

Prepare the goose. Brush the cavity with lemon juice. Insert stuffing (Basic Stuffing Page 79) and sew up the cavity. Melt the butter and shake in as much salt and pepper as desired. Brush the mixture over the outside of the goose.

Pour 2 cups (500 mL) water or juice into the bottom of a roasting pan. Arrange the goose on a rack in the pan, or somehow slightly off the bottom of the pan. Goose flesh sticks easily to the pan, and is hard to lift if not on a rack of some sort.

Bake uncovered in a 400ºF (200ºC) oven until light brown. Then turn the heat down to 325ºF (160ºC) and cook covered until tender — usually about 20 minutes per pound. If the goose is very fat, pierce the flesh with fork or skewer to release some of the fat. If the bird is tough, allow extra cooking time.

Baste frequently with the drippings. Wild birds are not as fat as the domestic type and tend to dry out during roasting.

ROAST PARTRIDGE

3 partridge	3 partridge
salt and pepper	salt and pepper
celery leaves or apple slices	celery leaves or apple slices
3 tsp. butter	15 mL butter
6 slices bacon	6 slices bacon
1 cup red wine or apple juice	250 mL red wine or apple juice
1 tbsp. cornstarch	15 mL cornstarch
¼ cup water	50 mL water

Prepare the birds. Pepper and salt the cavity and stuff with celery leaves and/or apple slices. Also put 1 tsp. (5 mL) butter in each cavity. Put into a roasting pan and cover the breasts with bacon. Roast uncovered in 350ºF (180ºC) oven for 15 minutes. Pour the wine or juice over the birds and continue baking another ½ hour, or until tender. Baste frequently.

Mix the 1 tbsp. (15 mL) cornstarch with ¼ cup (50 mL) water and stir until all lumps are gone. Add to the wine mixture in the roast and let cook until clear. Spoon over the birds and serve.

BAKED BEANS FROM SCRATCH

2 lbs. dried white navy beans	1 kg. dried white navy beans
1 tsp. baking soda	5 mL baking soda
½ lb. salt pork or bacon	250 g salt pork or bacon
1 medium onion, sliced	1 medium onion, sliced
2 tsp. salt	10 mL salt
4 tsp. cider vinegar	20 mL cider vinegar
3 tsp. prepared mustard	15 mL prepared mustard
¼ cup brown sugar, packed	50 mL brown sugar, packed
½ cup molasses	125 mL molasses
¼ cup ketchup	50 mL ketchup
black pepper to taste	black pepper to taste
1 can (10 oz.) tomato soup	1 can (284 mL) tomato soup

In a large pot, soak the beans overnight in water that is at least 3" (8 cm) above the beans. In the morning, drain and transfer the beans to your bean pot. Cover with fresh water to which the baking soda has been added. Add the salt pork or bacon, onion and salt. Bake for 2 hours in 325ºF (160ºC) oven or until slightly softened.

Then add vinegar, mustard, brown sugar, molasses, ketchup, pepper and tomato soup. Cover and bake in a 250ºF (120ºC) oven for 7-8 hours or until the beans are tender. If the liquid dries up during the baking process and the beans are not yet tender, add more water. (If you have tomato juice around, that works very well also.)

If you have a crock pot, you can use it instead of the oven. It uses electricity more efficiently than the oven but it doesn't fill the house with the aroma of baked beans.

BAKED BEAN CASSEROLE

½ lb. bacon, diced	250 g bacon, diced
½ lb. ground beef	250 g ground beef
½ cup onion, chopped	125 mL onion, chopped
¾ cup celery, chopped	175 mL celery, chopped
½ cup ketchup	125 mL ketchup
¼ cup brown sugar	50 mL brown sugar
1 tsp. dry mustard	5 mL dry mustard
2 tbsp. vinegar	25 mL vinegar
1 can (7 oz.) tomato sauce	1 can (198 g) tomato sauce
1 can (10 oz.) mushrooms, drained	1 can (284 mL) mushrooms, drained
2 cans (14 oz. each) pork & beans	2 can (398 mL each) pork & beans
1 can (14 oz.) kidney beans	1 can (398 mL) kidney beans

In large frying pan, cook bacon, ground beef and onion. Drain fat. Add remaining ingredients. Transfer to casserole. Bake uncovered in 350ºF (180ºC) oven for 45 minutes. Serves 8.

Beans were always an important part of the pioneer diet. One northern resident remembers how the hired man would get a can of beans from the house on his second last round in the field for that day.

He'd put the can on the manifold of the tractor and then complete the last round . . . by which time the beans would be hot enough for supper.

Before cans and corner stores came along, many early homemakers used to can their own pork and beans. One old recipe called for 12 pounds of dried beans and 10 pounds of fresh pork.

ALBERTA HOT POT

8 medium potatoes	8 medium potatoes
2 lbs. lean hamburger meat	1 kg lean hamburger meat
3 medium onions, sliced	3 medium onions, sliced
1 small turnip, sliced	1 small turnip, sliced
1 tsp. marjoram	5 mL marjoram
1 tbsp. salt	15 mL salt
dash of pepper	dash of pepper
2 tbsp. butter or margarine	25 mL butter or margarine
2 tbsp. chopped parsley	30 mL chopped parsley
1 cup beef broth*	250 mL beef broth*

Grease a large casserole dish, or small roaster. Peel and slice potatoes and place one third of them on the bottom of the pan. Top with one half of the meat, onion and turnip. Sprinkle with some of the marjoram, salt and pepper. Repeat layers, ending up with a final layer of potatoes. Dot with butter and sprinkle with parsley. Pour beef broth over all.

Bake covered in a 350ºF (180ºC) oven for 1½ hours or until potatoes are tender.

*Use homemade beef broth, or canned bouillon or powdered beef broth.

BACON TOPPED MACARONI

2 cups uncooked elbow macaroni	500 mL uncooked elbow macaroni
2 tbsp. butter	25 mL butter
3 tbsp. flour	50 mL flour
2½ cups milk	625 mL milk
½ lb. grated cheddar cheese	250 g grated cheddar cheese
salt and pepper	salt and pepper
1 tbsp. grated onion	15 mL grated onion
2 medium tomatoes, sliced	2 medium tomatoes, sliced
½ cup bread crumbs or croutons	125 mL bread crumbs or croutons
6-8 slices bacon, slightly fried	6-8 slices bacon, slightly fried

Cook the macaroni in boiling salted water until tender, about 8 minutes. Drain and rinse.

In a small saucepan, melt the butter and add the flour slowly, making a smooth paste. Add the milk slowly, stirring all the while until the sauce is smooth and thick. Add the cheese and seasonings.

In a large greased baking dish, pour the sauce over the macaroni. On top of the combination, layer the onion, tomatoes, crumbs and slightly fried bacon. Leave the bacon till the end because it flavours up the crumbs. Sprinkle more grated cheese over the casserole in the last 15 minutes of cooking. Bake for 30-40 minutes in 350°F (180°C) oven.

MEAT LOAF

1½ lbs. ground beef	750 g ground beef
2 cups cereal*	500 mL cereal*
2 eggs	2 eggs
1 cup milk	250 mL milk
3 tbsp. green onion, finely chopped	50 mL green onion, finely chopped
2 tsp. salt	10 mL salt
pepper	pepper
¼ tsp. dry mustard	1 mL dry mustard
¼ tsp. sage	1 mL sage

Mix the ingredients together and put in a greased loaf pan. If you want to turn the meat loaf out onto a plate, line the pan with foil first. Bake at 350°F (180°C) for 1½ hours.

TOPPING:

3 tbsp. brown sugar	50 mL brown sugar
¼ cup ketchup	50 mL ketchup
1 tsp. dry mustard	5 mL dry mustard
¼ tsp. nutmeg	1 mL nutmeg

Mix together and spread on the meat loaf ½ hour before it is done.

*You can use bran cereal or cornflakes or shredded shreddies or bread or cracker crumbs, or rolled oats.

REUBEN PIE

1 lb. lean ground beef	500 g lean ground beef
⅓ cup oatmeal	75 mL oatmeal
1 egg	1 egg
2 tbsp. worchestershire sauce	25 mL worcestershire sauce
2 tbsp. ketchup	25 mL ketchup
½ tsp. garlic powder	2 mL garlic powder
½ tsp. pepper	2 mL pepper
1 can (16 oz.) sauerkraut, drained	1 can (454 mL) sauerkraut, drained
2 cups shredded swiss cheese	500 mL shredded swiss cheese
1 tbsp. caraway seeds	15 mL caraway seeds
1 can (4 oz.) French fried onions*	1 can (125 g) French fried onions*

Mix meat, oatmeal, egg, worcestershire sauce, ketchup, garlic and pepper. Press into a 9" or 10" (23-25 cm) pie plate as a crust. Be sure to build up the sides all the way. Bake until the meat has lost its pinkness — about 20 minutes at 400°F (200°C). Pour off excess fat.

Meanwhile, mix the sauerkraut, cheese, caraway seeds and ⅓ of the onions. Pack firmly into the meat shell and bake another 20 minutes. Crumble the remaining onions on top and bake 5 more minutes. Serve immediately in pie shaped wedges.

*You may also use onion rings as found in the potato chip area sometimes. Otherwise, you might substitute potato chips . . . but the hint of onion is best. French fried onions come in cans in the supermarket now. Look for them in the potato chip section.

MEAT BALLS FOR COMPANY

½ loaf bread	½ loaf bread
2 lbs. lean ground beef	1 kg lean ground beef
1 cup grated romano cheese	250 mL grated romano cheese
6 eggs	6 eggs
½ cup crushed seasoned croutons*	125 mL crushed seasoned croutons*
1 tsp. parsley	5 mL parsley
garlic salt, salt & pepper to taste	garlic salt, salt and pepper to taste
4 tbsp. vegetable oil	50 mL vegetable oil
1 tin (10 oz.) mushroom soup	1 tin (284 mL) mushroom soup
1 cup sour cream	250 mL sour cream

Pour enough water over the sliced bread to soak and let sit for a minute; then squeeze out all the moisture. Discard the water. Break the bread into small pieces and add the hamburger, cheese, eggs, seasoned croutons, parsley and seasonings to taste. Mix well with hands.

Form into small balls and brown in hot oil. Remove from the pan as browned and put into a large casserole dish. When all the meatballs are done, drain excess fat from the pan and pour in the mushroom soup and sour cream. Heat to the boiling point, stirring up all the meat bits as you proceed. Pour the sauce over the meatballs in the casserole and bake in a 350°F (180°C) oven for about an hour. Keep the lid on.

*If you don't have croutons around, use another slice of bread.

MUGGSY'S SPAGHETTI SAUCE

4 lbs. ground beef	2 kg ground beef
2 medium onions, chopped	2 medium onions, chopped
1 can (7½ oz.) tomato sauce	1 can (213 mL) tomato sauce
1 can (10 oz.) tomato soup	1 can (284 mL) tomato soup
1 can (13 oz.) tomato paste	1 can (369 mL) tomato paste
1 can (28 oz.) tomatoes	1 can (786 mL) tomatoes
3 cups water	750 mL water
3 tsp. sugar	15 mL sugar
2 tsp. worcestershire sauce	10 mL worcestershire sauce
1 tsp. tabasco sauce	5 mL tabasco sauce
3 tsp. salt	15 mL salt
1½ tsp. oregano	7 mL oregano
1 tsp. garlic salt	5 mL garlic salt
1 tsp. basil	5 mL basil
1 tsp. celery salt	5 mL celery salt
½ tsp. pepper	2 mL pepper

In a large heavy pot, saute the meat and onions until all redness disappears from the meat and the onions are soft but not brown. Chop up the meat as it cooks. Add the remaining ingredients and simmer uncovered 2½-3 hours, stirring often.

Freeze in the quantity suitable for your family. If you haven't a pot large enough for this quantity, the recipe is easily halved. Use a smaller can of tomatoes plus the paste or soup — never mind the sauce. Otherwise, just reduce everything by half.

CABBAGE ROLLS

1 cabbage	1 cabbage
1 lb. sausage meat	500 g sausage meat
1 lb. lean ground beef	500 g lean ground beef
½ cup uncooked rice	125 mL uncooked rice
1 egg, beaten	1 egg, beaten
1 medium onion, chopped	1 medium onion, chopped
½ tsp. thyme	2 mL thyme
1 tsp. turmeric	5 mL turmeric
sprinkle of garlic salt	sprinkle of garlic salt
salt & pepper	salt & pepper
1 can (10 oz.) tomato soup	1 can (284 mL) tomato soup
1 can (10 oz.) water	1 can (284 mL) water
2 tbsp. vinegar	25 mL vinegar
sauerkraut (optional)	sauerkraut (optional)
bacon (optional)	bacon (optional)

Core the cabbage and steam for 15 minutes or so, until you can peel the leaves off without too much resistance. As you get toward the centre of the cabbage, you may have to steam that part a bit longer if the heat didn't penetrate all the way through. The leaves have to be limp enough to wrap around the meat and rice mixture.

Mix together the meats, rice, egg, onions, spices, garlic, salt and pepper. Place as much or as little as you want on a cabbage leaf. Fold the cabbage leaf around the mixture and secure with a toothpick. If you are trying to make small cabbage rolls, then cut some of the bigger cabbage leaves in half or use the smaller inside leaves. Don't wrap a lot of cabbage around a little bit of meat mixture.

Place the cabbage rolls in a heavy baking dish or a roaster. Mix together the soup, water and vinegar. Pour over the cabbage rolls and bake covered in 350°F (180°C) oven for about 2 hours.

Some people like an even stronger sour cabbage taste. If that is the case, layer the cabbage rolls with 1 can of sauerkraut. Then add the sauce and bake. The sauerkraut makes them taste a bit more "the way baba used to make them".

Bacon also adds a nice flavour. Cut up 4-5 pieces and scatter over the cabbage rolls before baking. They will add body and flavour.

ALL-IN-ONE-STEW

1 lb. stewing meat	500 g stewing meat
1 can (14 oz.) stewed tomatoes	1 can (398 mL) stewed tomatoes
1 cup frozen peas	250 mL frozen peas
¼ cup minute tapioca	50 mL minute tapioca
½ cup dry bread crumbs	125 mL dry bread crumbs
½ cup chopped celery	125 mL chopped celery
1 medium onion, chopped	1 medium onion, chopped
3 carrots, chopped	3 carrots, chopped
¼ lb. mushrooms*	250 g mushrooms*
salt & pepper to taste	salt & pepper to taste
pinch of basil	pinch of basil

Put the cut up stewing meat in the bottom of a good sized casserole or baking dish. Layer on top the tomatoes, peas, tapioca, bread crumbs, celery, onion, carrots, mushrooms. Season to taste with salt, pepper and basil.

Bake covered in 300°F (150°C) oven for 4-6 hours. Check every once in a while to make sure the mixture isn't too dry. Add water or tomato juice, if necessary.

*Use canned mushrooms in a pinch.

This sounds all too easy, but is remarkably good for the little work involved.

SWEET AND SOUR BEEF STEW

1½ lbs. beef stewing meat	750 g beef stewing meat
2 tbsp. vegetable oil	25 mL vegetable oil
1 cup chopped carrot	250 mL chopped carrot
1 cup sliced onion	250 mL sliced onion
1 can (8 oz.) tomato sauce	1 can (250 g) tomato sauce
¼ cup brown sugar	50 mL brown sugar
¼ cup vinegar	50 mL vinegar
1 tbsp. worcestershire sauce	15 mL worcestershire sauce
1 tsp. salt	5 mL salt
2 tbsp. cornstarch	25 mL cornstarch
½ cup cold water	125 mL cold water

Brown the meat in hot vegetable oil. Add the next 7 ingredients; cover and cook over low heat until the meat is tender — about 2 hours. (Or simmer in 325°F (160°C) oven for 2 hours).

Mix the cornstarch with the cold water until lumps have been worked out; then add to the bubbling beef mixture. Cook and stir until the gravy is thickened and bubbly.

Serve with noodles or rice.

FARMERS' STEW UPDATED

2 lbs. stewing beef, cubed	1 kg stewing beef, cubed
1 tbsp. butter	15 mL butter
1 tbsp. oil	15 mL oil
1 large onion, chopped	1 large onion, chopped
2 cloves garlic, minced	2 cloves garlic, minced
3 tbsp. flour	50 mL flour
1 can (10 oz.) beef broth	1 can (284 mL) beef broth
1 cup water	250 mL water
1 cup dry red wine	250 mL dry red wine
1 can (7 oz.) tomato sauce	1 can (198 g) tomato sauce
1 tbsp. chopped parsley	15 mL chopped parsley
½ tsp. dried crushed thyme	2 mL dried crushed thyme
1 small bay leaf	1 small bay leaf
salt & pepper to taste	salt & pepper to taste
4 medium carrots, sliced	4 medium carrots, sliced
2 small stalks celery, sliced	2 small stalks celery, sliced
fresh peas or beans	fresh peas or beans

In heavy pot or Dutch oven, brown meat in mixture of butter and oil. Add onion and garlic and cook until softened. Stir in flour. Add remaining ingredients except vegetables. Cover and bake in 325°F (160°C) oven for 2 hours or until beef is tender. Add vegetables and cook for about 45 minutes longer. Serve with boiled potatoes.

DILL STROGANOFF

1½ lbs. chuck steak or roast	750 g chuck steak or roast
¼ cup butter or margarine	50 mL butter or margarine
1 onion, chopped	1 onion, chopped
¼ lb. mushrooms, sliced	125 g mushrooms, sliced
3 tbsp. flour	50 mL flour
2 cups water	500 mL water
2 beef bouillon cubes*	2 beef bouillon cubes*
½ tsp. salt	2 mL salt
¼ tsp. pepper	1 mL pepper
1 cup sour cream	250 mL sour cream
2 tbsp. chopped fresh dill	25 mL chopped fresh dill
(or 1 tsp. dill weed)	(or 5 mL dill weed)

Cut the meat into long narrow strips and saute in a hot skillet with the butter or margarine just until the meat is brown on the outside. Remove with a slotted spoon and keep warm.

Add onions and mushrooms to the skillet and saute until golden. Stir in the flour, as for gravy, and then add the water. Let the sauce thicken and then add the instant beef flavouring, salt and pepper. Finally, add the sour cream and dill but do not let the mixture boil. Put meat back into the sauce and mix. Once again, heat through but do not boil. Serve with rice or noodles and garnish with more dill.

*Instead of beef bouillon cubes, you could use 2 tsp. (10 mL) instant beef broth.

BAKED ROUND STEAK

2 lb. round steak	1 kg round steak
¼ cup flour	50 mL flour
3 tbsp. shortening	50 mL shortening
½ envelope dry onion soup mix	½ envelope dry onion soup mix
½ cup water	125 mL water
1 can (10 oz.) mushroom soup	1 can (284 mL) mushroom soup

Sprinkle one side of meat with flour; pound in. Turn meat and repeat. Cut meat into servings.

Melt shortening in frying pan; brown meat over medium heat about 15 minutes.*

Mix onion soup mix, water and mushroom soup. Pour over meat. Cover tightly and simmer 1½ to 2 hours. Serves 4.

*At this point you can put meat into a casserole; add soup mixture and bake in 350°F (180°C) oven for 1½ hours.

OLD FASHIONED BEEF POT ROAST

4 lbs. beef chuck roast	2 kg beef chuck roast
2 tbsp. flour	30 mL flour
1 tbsp. oil	15 mL oil
2 tsp. salt	10 mL salt
¼ tsp. each of marjoram, thyme, basil and pepper	1 mL each of marjoram, thyme, basil and pepper
1 small onion, sliced	1 small onion, sliced
½ cup water	125 mL water
½ cup dry red wine	125 mL dry red wine
3 medium onions, cut in quarters	3 medium onions, cut in quarters
8 medium sized carrots	8 medium sized carrots
8 small potatoes, quartered	8 small potatoes, quartered
½ cup water	125 mL water

Sprinkle roast with flour and rub in. In a heavy pan, preferably a Dutch oven, brown the meat slowly on all sides in hot oil. Season with the salt and next 4 seasonings. Arrange the small onion slices over the roast; add the first ½ cup (125 mL) water and the wine. Cover and roast at 350°F (180°C) for 2 hours.

At that point, add the second ½ cup (125 mL) water and the vegetables. Cover again and cook for another hour, or until the vegetables are tender. Remove the cover occasionally and turn the potatoes so that all sides get browned in the juices. Remove the meat and vegetables to a platter and keep warm. Skim excess fat from the juices. Add water so that there is approximately 1½ cups (375 mL) liquid in the pan. Make a gravy by mixing together 3 tbsp. (50 mL) flour with ½ cup (125 mL) cold water. Stir until all lumps have gone. Pour slowly into the bubbling pan juices and stir like crazy so that new lumps don't appear. Simmer a few minutes. Season with salt and pepper to taste.

Pass the gravy with the meat.

Gravy was a very necessary commodity whenever potatoes were served, and since potatoes were just about always served, gravy ranked very high.

One old bachelor was equally fond of gravy and eating out. After every meal taken with neighbours or friends, he would say, "Thank you for the meal. It was very good and , Lady, the gravy was excellent!"

PORK ROAST

5 lb. boneless pork roast	2.5 kg boneless pork roast
½ cup soy sauce	125 mL soy sauce
¼ cup dry sherry or fruit juice	50 mL dry sherry or fruit juice
½ cup brown sugar	125 mL brown sugar
¼ tsp. ginger	1 mL ginger
1 medium onion, chopped	1 medium onion, chopped
1 clove garlic, minced	1 clove garlic, minced

In a bowl big enough to hold the roast, mix together the soy sauce, sherry or fruit juice, brown sugar, ginger, onion and garlic. Place the roast in the bowl, turning to coat with the marinade. Refrigerate, covered, for several hours or overnight, turning the roast occasionally or basting it.

Remove the roast and put onto a rack in the roaster. Without a rack the marinated bottom of the roast might stick to the roaster. Roast, uncovered, at 325°F (160°C) for 2½-3 hours. Bring out the marinade in the last half hour of roasting and pour it over the meat, basting frequently until done.

You can make a gravy out of the marinade that remains after the roast is finished, or you can serve it up as a sauce. To make gravy, skim off excess fat and add a mixture of 2 tbsp. (30 mL) flour mixed with 1 cup (250 mL) water. Stir until the mixture is smooth and thick.

BARBECUE SAUCE

1 bottle ketchup (11 oz.)	1 bottle ketchup (313 mL)
2 tbsp. vinegar	25 mL vinegar
salt & pepper to taste	salt & pepper to taste
1 tsp. worcestershire sauce	5 mL worcestershire sauce
5 drops tabasco sauce	5 drops tabasco sauce
1 medium onion, chopped	1 medium onion, chopped
2 tsp. dry mustard	10 mL dry mustard
1 clove garlic, minced	1 clove garlic, minced

Combine the ingredients in a medium sized saucepan and simmer 30 minutes.

Use for barbecuing steaks, chicken or spare ribs.

BARBECUE SPARERIBS

Spareribs, as many as you need
Barbecue sauce, as on page 61

Precook the spareribs by placing in a roaster with a little water and baking for at least one hour. Some of the excess fat is thus boiled out. Drain the liquid off the ribs but save a bit in case you need to thin the sauce a bit.

Make barbecue sauce as instructed above and pour over the ribs. Cover and bake 1½ hours. If the sauce gets too thick, cut it with a bit of the liquid drained from the first process.

Remove to serving plates and pass the serviettes. This is finger work.

SWEET AND SOUR SAUCE

½ cup water	125 mL water
½ cup brown sugar	125 mL brown sugar
¼ cup vinegar	50 mL vinegar
¼ cup ketchup	50 mL ketchup
1½ tbsp. cornstarch	20 mL cornstarch
1 tbsp. soy sauce	15 mL soy sauce

Put all ingredients into a small saucepan and cook until thick and clear.

Use for sweet and sour spareribs or as a glaze for ham or as a sauce for pork chops. This is a good basic no-nonsense sauce.

SWEET AND SOUR SPARERIBS

Spare ribs, as many as you need
Sweet and sour sauce, from above

Put the ribs into a roaster with a bit of water, put the lid on and bake for an hour at 350°F (180°C). The idea is to boil out the excess fat. After an hour, drain off the liquid.

Then pour the sweet and sour sauce over the ribs and bake another hour at 350°F (180°C). Keep the lid on so the ribs can get as tender and finger lickin' good as possible.

The recipe for sweet and sour sauce above would make enough sauce for 4 servings. If you are having more or less, adjust the recipe accordingly.

At the last minute, add drained pineapple rings or chunks. Sprinkle fresh green onions over the ribs.

A Picnic in the Country

Counterclockwise from the picnic basket:
Basic White Bread and Whole Wheat Bread
Potato Salad With Peas
Rhubarb Pie
Fried Chicken
Baked Bean Casserole
Fran's Corned Beef
Tomato Aspic

FRAN'S CORNED BEEF

1 pkg. uncooked corned beef	1 pkg. uncooked corned beef
2 whole cloves	2 whole cloves
1 medium onion, chopped	1 medium onion, chopped
1 celery stalk, chopped	1 celery stalk, chopped
3 tsp. vegetable oil	15 mL vegetable oil
1 tbsp. prepared mustard	15 mL prepared mustard
¼ cup brown sugar	50 mL brown sugar
⅓ cup chili sauce	75 mL chili sauce
¼ cup cider vinegar	50 mL cider vinegar
¼ cup cold water	50 mL cold water

Follow the instructions on the covering of the corned beef concerning the boiling of the meat. While boiling, add the cloves, onion and celery and cook until tender.

When the meat is done, lift from pan and transfer to a baking dish. Combine the oil, mustard, brown sugar, chili sauce, vinegar and cold water. Pour over the cooked meat and bake at 350°F (180°C) for 30 minutes. Baste with the sauce several times.

Serve with boiled new potatoes, or cabbage done in a favourite way.

DORIS' SWEET & SOUR PORK

1½-2 lbs. short ribs (pork)
¼ cup water
1 can (14 oz.) pineapple chunks
¼ cup brown sugar
2 tbsp. cornstarch
¼ cup vinegar
2-3 tbsp. soy sauce
½ tsp. salt
1 small green pepper
¼ cup sliced onion

750 g-1 kg short ribs (pork)
50 mL water
1 can (398 mL) pineapple chunks
50 mL brown sugar
30 mL cornstarch
50 mL vinegar
30-50 mL soy sauce
2 mL salt
1 small green pepper
50 mL sliced onion

Brown pork in fry pan. Add ¼ cup (50 mL) water. Cover and simmer 1 hour. (Alternative — transfer ribs to casserole or roaster and bake at 350ºF (180ºC) for 1 hour).

Drain pineapple and reserve syrup. Combine sugar, cornstarch, pineapple syrup, vinegar, soy sauce and salt.

Drain fat from pork. Add the sauce mixture and cook on top of stove, until sauce thickens, stirring often. Add pineapple, green pepper and onion. Cook 2-3 minutes.

Serve with hot rice. Serves 4.

TOURTIERE

pastry for 2 pies
2 lbs. lean hamburger
½ lb. ground pork
1½ cups hot water
1½ tsp. salt
¼ tsp. pepper
1 large onion, chopped
1 sprig celery leaves
½ tsp. allspice
dash of cloves
1 large peeled potato

pastry for 2 pies
1 kg lean hamburger
250 g ground pork
375 mL hot waer
7 mL salt
1 mL pepper
1 large onion, chopped
1 sprig celery leaves
2 mL allspice
dash of cloves
1 large peeled potato

In a heavy pot, combine all the ingredients except for the potato. Bring to a boil. Reduce heat and simmer, covered, for half an hour. Add the whole potato and cook gently another hour. Discard the potato and the celery leaves. Cool the meat mixture.

When it is cooled, line 2 regular sized pie plates with pastry. The regular basic pastry recipe on page 157 works fine for this purpose. Spoon the meat mixture into the shells, cover with a top layer of pastry in which slits have been cut for the escape of steam, seal and bake in 375ºF (190ºC) oven for 45 minutes or until pastry is well browned.

PORK CHOP CASSEROLE

4 pork chops
4 potatoes
salt and pepper to taste
2 medium onions, sliced
1 can (14 oz.) kernel corn
1 can (10 oz.) mushroom soup
1 cup milk

4 pork chops
4 potatoes
salt and pepper to taste
2 medium onions, sliced
1 can (398 mL) kernel corn
1 can (284 mL) mushroom soup
250 mL milk

Essentially, this is a layering of potatoes, onion, corn and pork chops with a suitable amount of soup and milk poured over top.

Brown the pork chops. Grease a large casserole or baking dish and layer the sliced potatoes on the bottom. Sprinkle with a little salt and pepper. Then layer with the onions and the kernel corn. Finally, lay the pork chops on top and cover with soup and milk mixed together.

Bake at 350°F (180°C) for about 2 hours.

If you have a bigger or smaller family, judge accordingly.

HAM PASTIES

pie crust from recipe on Page 157

pie crust from recipe on Page 157

FILLING:
3 cups finely diced cooked ham
2 tbsp. chopped green pepper
2 tbsp. chopped pimento
1 tbsp. minced onion
1 can (10 oz.) mushroom soup

FILLING:
750 mL finely diced cooked ham
30 mL chopped green pepper
30 mL chopped pimento
15 mL minced onion
1 can (284 mL) mushroom soup

TOPPING:
1 egg, beaten
1 tbsp. water
poppy seed, caraway seeds
   or sesame seeds

TOPPING:
1 egg, beaten
15 mL water
poppy seeds, caraway seeds
   or sesame seeds

Roll out portions of the dough on lightly floured surface to ⅛" (3 mm) thickness. Cut into circles approximately 4" (10 cm) in diameter. Place circles on ungreased baking sheets. Prepare the filling, by combining all 5 ingredients. Spread a tablespoon of filling on half of pastry. Moisten edge and fold over. Seal edges with tines of fork. Cut slits in tops of pasties for steam to escape. Brush pasties with mixture of egg and water.

Sprinkle poppy seeds, caraway seeds or sesame seeds over top if desired.

Bake at 400°F (200°C) for 15-20 minutes or until golden brown. Serve warm.

Note: Pasties may be baked and frozen, to be reheated before serving; or they may be frozen unbaked.

LIVER, BACON & ONION CASSEROLE

¼ cup flour	50 mL flour
½ tsp. salt	2 mL salt
¼ tsp. pepper	1 mL pepper
1 lb. beef liver	500 g beef liver
6 slices bacon	6 slices bacon
1 onion	1 onion
1 can (10 oz.) tomato soup	1 can (284 mL) tomato soup
¾ cup water	175 mL water

Mix flour and seasonings. Set aside.

Fry bacon until done but not crisp. Drain on paper towelling. Slice onion and fry rings in bacon fat. Drain on paper towelling.

Dip liver into flour mixture. Coat all over on both sides. Brown in frying pan in remaining bacon drippings. Brown on both sides. Transfer liver to a 1½ quart (1.5 L) casserole. Place onions on top of liver and bacon on top.

Mix tomato soup with water. Pour over liver and bake in 350ºF (180ºC) oven for about 40 minutes.

FRIED CHICKEN

½ cup flour	125 mL flour
1 tsp. salt	5 mL salt
1 tsp. paprika	5 mL paprika
pinch of pepper	pinch of pepper
shortening or vegetable oil	shortening or vegetable oil
1 fryer chicken, cut up	1 fryer chicken, cut up

Mix flour and seasonings in a paper or plastic bag. Add chicken pieces a few at a time and shake until well coated.

Heat shortening or oil ½" (1 cm) deep in a skillet over medium heat. Place chicken pieces in the hot oil, skin side down first. Cook, uncovered, 15-20 minutes per side, turning only once. Drain on paper towels.

GRAVY

2 tbsp. shortening or oil from frying process	25 mL shortening or oil left from frying process
2 tbsp. flour	30 mL flour
1½ cups milk or water	375 mL milk or water
salt and pepper to taste	salt and pepper to taste

Drain shortening or oil from the skillet, leaving only 2 tbsp. (25 mL). Sprinkle flour over the oil and drippings. Return to heat and gradually add the liquid and salt and pepper as desired. Cook until thickened. Serve hot.

QUICK CHICKEN DISH

1 chicken, cut up	1 chicken, cut up
1 can (10 oz.) mushroom soup	1 can (284 mL) mushroom soup
1 can (10 oz.) celery soup	1 can (284 mL) celery soup
1 can (10 oz.) cream of chicken soup	1 can (284 mL) cream of chicken soup
2 cups milk	500 mL milk
1½ cups uncooked rice	375 mL uncooked rice
1 pkg. dry onion soup mix	1 pkg. dry onion soup mix

Grease a 13 x 9" (3.5 L) baking dish.

In a medium sized saucepan, heat the first three soups with the milk. Pour into the bottom of the baking dish. Sprinkle the rice evenly over the soup mixture. Arrange the chicken pieces on that and finally shake the onion soup mix over everything.

Bake for 2 hours at 325°F (160°C).

After the war, canned soups became popular. They would be added to stews, roasts, liver and onions, casseroles, vegetable dishes . . . even cakes! (See page 125).

The Quick Chicken Dish (above) is the ultimate in soup can cooking . . . it uses a total of four different prepared soups. But the result is both good tasting and good looking.

Nobody could guess by looking at it or tasting it that it's as simple as it actually is!

CURRIED CHICKEN

4 tbsp. butter or margarine	50 mL butter or margarine
½ cup honey	125 mL honey
¼ cup prepared mustard*	50 mL prepared mustard*
1 tsp. salt	5 mL salt
1 tsp. curry powder	5 mL curry powder
3 lbs. chicken cut up	1.5 kg chicken, cut up

Melt the butter or margarine in a baking dish. Stir in the honey, mustard, salt and curry powder. Wipe each piece of chicken and then roll in the mixture in the pan, making sure that all sides get coated with the mixture. Place meaty side up and bake uncovered for 1 hour in 375°F (190°C) oven. Turn occasionally, and baste.

*You can use 1 tsp. (5 mL) dry mustard here, with a bit of water.

CHICKEN TERIYAKI

1 whole chicken, cut up	1 whole chicken, cut up
¼ tsp. ginger	1 mL ginger
1 clove garlic, minced	1 clove garlic, minced
½ cup dry white wine*	125 mL dry white wine*
½-1 cup light soy sauce**	125-250 mL light soy sauce**
¼ cup sugar	50 mL sugar

Marinate chicken pieces in soy sauce which has been spiced and sweetened with sugar, wine, garlic and ginger. It takes some stirring to dissolve sugar in soy sauce. Marinate at least 2 hours.

Spread chicken on a fairly large shallow pan and bake in 350°F (180°C) oven for about 40 minutes. Turn at half time and baste. Baste often with the sauce mixture and chicken will have a glaze when finished. Serve with steamed rice.

*Dry white wine is optional.

**If you only have the heavy traditional soy sauce, use the lesser amount and add a bit of water.

CHICKEN IN MUSTARD SAUCE

¼ cup flour	50 mL flour
½ tsp. salt	2 mL salt
¼ tsp. garlic powder	1 mL garlic powder
¼ tsp. onion flakes	1 mL onion flakes
2 chicken breasts, skinned and boned or 1-1½ lbs. chicken cutlets	2 chicken breasts, skinned and boned or 500-700 g chicken cutlets
2 tbsp. margarine	25 mL margarine
1 tsp. chicken in a mug or 1 chicken bouillon cube	15 mL chicken in a mug or 1 chicken bouillon cube
¾ cup water	175 mL water
½ tbsp. lemon juice	7 mL lemon juice
¾ tsp. dry mustard	3 mL dry mustard
1 tsp. sugar	5 mL sugar
½ tbsp. cornstarch	7 mL cornstarch
1 tbsp. water	15 mL water

Mix first 4 ingredients. Coat chicken with this mixture and saute in margarine about 5-10 minutes. Add next 2 ingredients; cover and simmer 30 minutes. Remove chicken to warm platter. Blend remaining ingredients and stir into chicken broth to make a gravy. Pour over chicken. Makes 3-4 servings.

Most farms kept a few chickens (anywhere from 10-200, depending on the proximity of coyotes!). Geese and ducks were also common, with the geese ruling the roost and chasing little kids and dogs at every opportunity.

The fowl were generally reserved for company meals. Kids in the family were always carefully instructed beforehand that they could only have what was left — after the company had had first choice. Consequently, we seldom made the acquaintance of a drumstick or thigh. Those desirable portions would be long gone before the chicken or duck made it to the kids' end of the table.

The wings and the pope's nose were more likely to be our portions.

TURKEY PIE

pastry for 9" pie —
   top layer only
3 tbsp. butter or margarine
1 medium onion, sliced
1 tbsp. sliced green pepper
1 can (10 oz.) mushroom soup
½ cup milk
2 cups chopped cooked turkey*
¾ cup cooked vegetables**
½ tsp. salt
dash of pepper

pastry for 23 cm pie —
   top layer only
50 mL butter or margarine
1 medium onion, sliced
15 mL sliced green pepper
1 can (284 mL) mushroom soup
125 mL milk
500 mL chopped cooked turkey*
175 mL cooked vegetables**
2 mL salt
dash of pepper

In fairly large frypan or baking dish, saute the onions and green pepper in the butter or margarine. Add the soup, milk, meat, vegetables and salt and pepper.

Pour into a large pie plate. Roll pastry out; make suitable slits to let the steam escape and arrange over the hot meat mixture in the pie plate. Seal and flute the edge. Bake in 425°F (220°C) oven for about half an hour — until the pastry is done.

*You can also use chicken instead of turkey

**Use whatever vegetables you have left over or use a few frozen vegetables.

CORNISH GAME HENS, I DARE YOU

½ cup sherry or orange juice
½ cup soy sauce
¼ cup cooking oil
1 tbsp. dry mustard
2 tbsp. water
2 cornish game hens, cut in
   half lengthwise

125 mL sherry or orange juice
125 mL soy sauce
50 mL cooking oil
15 mL dry mustard
25 mL water
2 cornish game hens, cut in
   half lengthwise

Get the butcher to cut the hens in half or tackle the job at home. Mix together the sherry or juice, soy sauce and oil.

In a smaller container, make a paste of the dry mustard and water and then add to the other liquids. Marinate the game hens in the mixture for 24 hours, turning as often as you remember. Keep in refrigerator until ready to cook.

When meal time approaches, broil the hens about 6" (15 cm) from the heat for at least 15 minutes on each side. Start with the cut side. Baste with marinade occasionally.

The birds turn an irresistible brown and the meat stays juicy and tender.

BAKED STUFFED FISH

3-4 pound fish	1.5-2 kg fish
2 tbsp. butter	25 mL butter
¼ cup chopped onion	50 mL chopped onion
¼ cup chopped celery	50 mL chopped celery
1 cup rolled oats	250 mL rolled oats
1 cup soft bread crumbs	250 mL soft bread crumbs
1 tsp. salt	5 mL salt
½ tsp. dill weed	2 mL dill weed
1 egg, beaten	1 egg, beaten
¼ cup water	50 mL water
1 tbsp. melted butter	15 mL melted butter
½ tsp. paprika	2 mL paprika

Clean and prepare fish. For the dressing, melt the butter in a fry pan. Add the onion and celery and brown lightly.

In another bowl, mix together the rolled oats, bread crumbs, salt and dill weed. Beat the egg lightly with the ¼ cup (50 mL) water. Add to the bread crumb mixture. Also add the celery and onion mixture. Toss lightly.

Sprinkle the inside of the fish with ½ tsp. (2 mL) salt. Then fill the cavity with the dressing - do not pack too tightly. Close opening with skewers or thread and place in a greased shallow baking pan.

Brush the fish with the melted butter and shake paprika on lightly. Bake in 350°F (180°C) oven for 30-35 minutes, just until the fish flakes lightly when poked. Baste occasionally.

Serve with Yogurt Dill Sauce.

YOGURT DILL SAUCE

1 cup plain yogurt	250 mL plain yogurt
1 tbsp. vegetable oil	15 mL vegetable oil
1 small cucumber, pared & diced	1 small cucumber pared & diced
1 tbsp. fresh dill, chopped or	15 mL fresh dill, chopped or
1 tsp. dried dill weed	5 ml dried dill weed
dash of salt	dash of salt
dash of freshly ground pepper	dash of freshly ground pepper

Combine everything in a small bowl and cover. Chill for at least 2 hours.

Serve with baked fish or barbecued fish, or use as a dressing for a salad which includes fish.

TUNA CASSEROLE

1 tin (7 oz.) flaked tuna	1 tin (220 g) flaked tuna
1 cup crushed potato chips	250 mL crushed potato chips
1 tin (10 oz.) mushroom soup	1 tin (284 mL) mushroom soup
½ cup milk	125 mL milk
1 cup peas (frozen are best)	250 mL peas (frozen are best)

Drain the tuna and crush the potato chips. There is no need to cook the peas first. Put all five ingredients into a greased baking dish and top with more crushed potato chips.

Bake in 350°F (180°C) oven for about an hour.

Kids in the fifties and sixties grew up on tuna casserole. It was a classic case of soup can cooking . . . and like all classics, has worn the years gracefully.

Salmon casserole (following) is in the same classical mold — quick, easy, nutritious and delicious.

SALMON CASSEROLE

2 cups noodles	500 mL noodles
3 cups water	750 mL water
1 can (10 oz.) mushroom soup	1 can (284 mL) mushroom soup
½ cup milk	125 mL milk
1 cup cubed cheddar cheese	250 mL cubed cheddar cheese
1 can (7¾ oz.) salmon, drained	1 can (220 g) salmon, drained
crushed cornflakes or Chinese noodles	crushed cornflakes or Chinese noodles

Cook noodles in water until tender (about 8-10 minutes). Drain.

Heat the soup and milk in saucepan and when blended add cheese. Stir until cheese is melted.

Combine the salmon, noodles and cheese sauce. Pour into greased casserole dish. Top with cornflakes or Chinese noodles.

Bake at 325°F (160°C) for 20 minutes. Makes 4 servings.

FISH CASSEROLE

4 pieces (approx. 1½ lbs.) white fish
salt and pepper to taste
1 cup fresh mushrooms
1 cup grated Jack cheese*
2 diced green onions
2 stalks celery, chopped
chopped parsley

4 pieces (approx. 750 g) white fish
salt and pepper to taste
250 mL fresh mushrooms
250 mL grated Jack cheese*
2 diced green onions
2 stalks celery, chopped
chopped parsley

Place fish in lightly oiled dish. Lightly salt and pepper. On top of the fish layer mushrooms, cheese, onion, celery and parsley. Bake at 350°F (180°C) for 30 minutes. Serves 4.

*If you can't find Jack cheese, use a white cheddar cheese.

SIMPLE SHRIMP CREOLE

¼ cup butter or margarine
½ cup finely chopped onion
½ cup finely chopped green pepper
1 small garlic clove, minced
1 can (14 oz.) tomatoes
6-8 ozs. precooked shrimp

50 mL butter or margarine
125 mL finely chopped onion
125 mL finely chopped green pepper
1 small garlic clove, minced
1 can (398 mL) tomatoes
227 mL precooked shrimp

In a saucepan, melt the butter or margarine until frothy and add the onion, green pepper and garlic. Cook until the vegetables are limp but not lost. Add the tomatoes. Simmer for 20 minutes or so, uncovered.

Add the shrimp. Heat through — 5 minutes or so. Serve over rice.

CRUSTLESS QUICHE

3 eggs
½ cup prepared biscuit mix
½ cup melted butter
1½ cups milk
dash of nutmeg, salt & pepper
1 cup shredded Swiss cheese*
½ cup cooked bacon or ham

3 eggs
125 mL prepared biscuit mix
125 mL melted butter
375 mL milk
dash of nutmeg, salt & pepper
250 mL shredded Swiss cheese*
125 mL cooked bacon or ham

Put all ingredients except the meat and cheese into the blender and whirl until well mixed. Pour into a greased large pie plate or quiche dish. Sprinkle the meat and cheese on top and then with a spoon, push the meat and cheese below the surface of the egg mixture.

Bake at 350ºF (180ºC) for 45 minutes or until knife inserted into centre comes out clean. Let sit 10 minutes before cutting. Tastes good reheated the next day as well.

*You can use cheddar cheese as well.

By some magic, this forms its own crust.

CRAB QUICHE

½ cup mayonnaise	125 mL mayonnaise
2 tbsp. flour	30 mL flour
2 eggs, beaten	2 eggs, beaten
½ cup milk	125 mL milk
1½ cups crabmeat (7½ oz. can)	220 g crabmeat
8 oz. Swiss cheese, grated	250 g Swiss cheese, grated
¼ cup sliced green onion	50 mL sliced green onion

Blend together the mayonnaise, flour, eggs and milk. Fold in the crab, cheese and green onion.

Pour into 9" (23 cm) pie plate or quiche pan (no crust). Bake at 350ºF (180ºC) for 40-45 minutes or until knife inserted into the centre comes out clean.

EGG BLITZ FOR BREAKFAST OR BRUNCH

8 slices of bread	8 slices of bread
softened butter	softened butter
garlic powder or salt	garlic powder or salt
1 tbsp. minced green onion	15 mL minced green onion
1 lb. sharp cheddar cheese, grated	500 g sharp cheddar cheese, grated
6 eggs	6 eggs
3 cups milk	750 mL milk
½ tsp. salt	2 mL salt
¾ tsp. dry mustard	3 mL dry mustard
½ tsp. pepper	2 mL pepper
1 tbsp. worcestershire sauce	15 mL worcestershire sauce

Butter the bread; sprinkle with garlic salt or powder and cut into ½" (1 cm) cubes. Grease an 8 x 8" (2 L) cake pan and place half the bread crumbs in the bottom of the pan. Cover with half the cheese and the onion. Repeat the bread and cheese layers. Mix remaining ingredients in blender (or with a mixer) and pour over the bread. Cover and refrigerate overnight.

An hour before breakfast or brunch time, take the cover off and bake in a 350ºF (180ºC) oven for about 1 hour. The dish will be puffy and golden. Serve immediately.

EGGS TO GET UP FOR

2 tbsp. vegetable oil
½ cup chopped celery
¼ cup chopped green pepper
¼ cup finely chopped onion
1 can (10 oz.) cream of celery soup
½ cup milk
1 cup diced process cheese*
4 hard boiled eggs
olives (optional)

25 mL vegetable oil
125 mL chopped celery
50 mL chopped green pepper
50 mL finely chopped onion
1 can (284 mL) cream of celery soup
125 mL milk
250 mL diced process cheese*
4 hard boiled eggs
olives (optional)

In a medium saucepan, heat the vegetable oil and saute the celery, green pepper and onion until tender. Add the soup, milk and cheese. Heat and stir until cheese is melted.

Cut the hard boiled eggs into quarters or slices. Add to the cheese mixture. Spoon over hot buttered toast or crumpets or English muffins. Garnish with olives, if desired.

*You may substitute a cheese spread, or grated cheddar cheese of the mild variety.

PUFFY OMELET

4 egg whites
4 egg yolks
1 tbsp. butter or margarine
2 tbsp. cold water
dash of salt

4 egg whites
4 egg yolks
15 mL butter or margarine
25 mL cold water
dash of salt

Beat egg whites until frothy; add cold water and dash of salt. Beat until stiff peaks form.

Beat egg yolks until thick and lemon colored. Fold yolks into whites.

Melt butter in a 10" (25 cm) oven proof fry pan — cast iron is good. Pour in the egg mixture, spread to the edges of the pan, leaving the sides of the pan with a light build up. Reduce heat. Cook until puffed and bottom is golden — about 7 minutes.

Bake in a 325ºF (160ºC) oven until knife inserted in the centre comes out clean, about another 7 minutes. Loosen sides of the omelet and score the omelet somewhat in half. In other words, one half should be bigger than the other. Fold the smaller half over the bigger half and slip out onto a warm plate.

THE VEGETABLE GARDEN PIE

1 cup whole wheat flour	250 mL whole wheat flour
1 cup white flour	250 mL white flour
1 tsp. salt	5 mL salt
⅔ cup shortening	150 mL shortening
5-7 tbsp. cold water	60-100 mL cold water

FILLING:

1 cup chopped zucchini	250 mL chopped zucchini
1 cup chopped celery	250 mL chopped celery
½ cup shredded carrot	125 mL shredded carrot
½ cup sliced mushroom	125 mL sliced mushroom
½ cup chopped green pepper	125 mL chopped green pepper
1 clove garlic, minced	1 clove garlic, minced
2 tbsp. cooking oil	25 mL cooking oil
1 can (14 oz.) tomato sauce	1 can (398 mL) tomato sauce
1 cup cooked vegetables*	250 mL cooked vegetables*
1 tbsp. brown sugar	15 mL brown sugar
1 tsp. dried oregano	5 mL dried oregano
1 tsp. chili powder	5 mL chili powder
½ tsp. salt	2 mL salt
½ tsp. basil	2 mL basil
dash of pepper	dash of pepper
dash of allspice	dash of allspice
1 cup shredded cheddar cheese	250 mL shredded cheddar cheese
1 egg, beaten	1 egg, beaten
1 tbsp. water	15 mL water

Stir together the flours and salt. Cut in the shortening until the mixture resembles coarse crumbs. Add the cold water and form into pastry. Line a 9" or 10" (23-25 cm) pie plate.

In a large Dutch oven or skillet, fry the zucchini, celery, carrots, mushrooms, green pepper and garlic in hot oil until the vegetables are just barely tender — 3 or 5 minutes. Add tomato sauce, cooked vegetables, sugar and seasonings. Cook another 5 minutes. Put the vegetable mixture into the prepared pastry and cover with shredded cheese. Cover with pastry. Leave slits in the pastry or a design so that the steam can escape. Mix the beaten egg with the 1 tbsp. water and brush the top of the pastry. This gives a shiny brown finish to the pie.

Bake at 350°F (180°C) until the pastry is done, about 30-40 minutes.

*Example: green beans, kernel corn, chopped broccoli.

The sod roof was a dubious blessing. It did keep the cold and wind out, but when it rained outside for a day, it continued to rain inside for another week.

PILAF WITHOUT PAIN

2 tbsp. margarine or butter	25 mL butter or margarine
1 cup uncooked rice	250 mL uncooked rice
4 green onions	4 green onions
1 tin (10 oz.) consomme*	1 tin (284 mL) consomme*
1 tin (10 oz.) mushrooms & juice	1 tin (284 mL) mushrooms & juice
1 tin (10 oz.) water	1 tin (284 mL) water
1 tsp. oregano	5 mL oregano
salt & pepper to taste	salt & pepper to taste

Heat the margarine or butter in a heavy fry pan and stir in the uncooked rice and green onions. Brown both. Add the other ingredients and transfer to a greased baking dish. Bake at 325°F (160°C) for one hour.

This is an easy basic pilaf. Add cooked chicken, shrimp or other meats, if desired, at the end of the cooking period, or throughout the cooking period, for that matter. Also, fresh mushrooms are nice. If you want to use them, fry along with the uncooked rice and green onions. Add ½ cup (125 mL) extra liquid.

*You can use the reconstituted cube or powder type here as well.

CURRIED ORANGE RICE

¼ cup margarine*	50 mL margarine*
1 medium onion, sliced thinly	1 medium onion, sliced thinly
1½ tsp. curry powder	7 mL curry powder
1 cup uncooked rice	250 mL uncooked rice
1 cup orange juice	250 mL orange juice
1 cup chicken broth	250 mL chicken broth
1 tsp. salt	5 mL salt
½ cup raisins	125 mL raisins
1 bay leaf	1 bay leaf

Melt margarine in saucepan. Saute onion until golden and soft. Stir in curry and rice. Cook 2 minutes, stirring constantly.

Add remaining ingredients, stir with fork. Bring to boil. Lower heat and cover. Let stand on minimum heat 15-20 minutes until rice is tender and liquid absorbed. Remove bay leaf before serving. Serves 4-6.

This recipe may be easily halved. Serve with chicken or pork chops.

*Reduce the amount of margarine if you use a non-stick pan.

BASIC STUFFING (for fowl)

4 tbsp. butter or margarine	50 mL butter or margarine
¼ cup onion, chopped	50 mL onion, chopped
¼ cup celery, chopped	50 mL celery, chopped
2 cups bread crumbs	500 mL bread crumbs
1 tbsp. lemon juice	15 mL lemon juice
½ tsp. salt	2 mL salt
dash of pepper	dash of pepper

Melt the butter or margarine in a large skillet. Add the onion and celery and heat briefly. Stir in the bread crumbs. Add remaining ingredients and mix thoroughly. If dressing seems dry, add 1 tbsp. (15 mL) water or milk to moisten.

VARIATIONS:

Dressing can be varied according to your imagination and cupboard. In fact, that's the appeal of it.

Try 1 cup mushrooms (250 mL) added with the onion and celery.

Add sage and/or poultry dressing according to taste.

Add chopped up apple and raisins along with the bread crumbs.

If the bird is big, increase ingredients as necessary. Stuffing can always be stretched by increasing the amount of bread crumbs.

DRESSING FOR WILD FOWL

2 tbsp. oil	25 mL oil
1 large onion, chopped	1 large onion, chopped
2 cups bread crumbs	500 mL bread crumbs
1 cup oatmeal	250 mL oatmeal
1 tsp. sage and/or poultry seasoning	5 mL sage and/or poultry seasoning
salt & pepper to taste	salt & pepper to taste
¼ cup water	50 mL water

Heat the oil in a fry pan and cook the onion until limp. Mix in the bread crumbs, oatmeal, sage and/or poultry seasoning, salt, pepper and water. Place into cavity of prepared bird.

This particular dressing, with the addition of the oatmeal would take a fairly long time to cook through so it would be best to use it in larger fowl, such as ducks or geese, if anybody gets wild geese anymore. You could use it in a small roast chicken as well.

RICE DRESSING

2 tbsp. butter	25 mL butter
1 cup uncooked minute rice	250 mL uncooked minute rice
2 cups cold water	500 mL cold water
1 tsp. salt	5 mL salt
3 tbsp. butter	50 mL butter
1 medium onion, chopped	1 medium onion, chopped
2 tbsp. dry parsley	30 mL dry parsley
⅔ cup diced celery	150 mL diced celery
½ tsp. thyme	2 mL thyme
½ tsp. sage	2 ml sage
2 eggs, well beaten	2 eggs, well beaten
2 cups bread crumbs	500 mL bread crumbs
salt & pepper to taste	salt & pepper to taste

Take 2 tbsp. (25 mL) butter and melt in large heavy saucepan. Brown the uncooked rice in it. Add the water and salt. Bring to a boil and simmer for 10 minutes, or until the rice is quite thoroughly cooked. There should be no water remaining.

Add the rest of the butter, the onion, parsley, celery, spices, eggs, bread crumbs, salt and pepper. Place in the cavity of a prepared bird. (Do you suppose any bird is prepared to be stuffed?)

One day a farm woman brought some butter into the general store in Nampa. She asked the storekeeper if she could trade her butter for someone else's since a mouse had fallen into her cream and the family wanted no part of that particular batch of butter.

However, another family who didn't know about the mouse wouldn't know the difference, she pointed out to the storekeeper.

So, he took her butter downstairs and brought an equal amount back up and she happily took it all back home again. What she didn't know was that he brought her own butter back up and she took home exactly what she had brought.

It was too good a joke to keep quiet about so the storekeeper asked her one day how she and her family had liked the substitute butter. Fine, she said.

"It just goes to show," she said, "that what you don't know doesn't hurt you."

The storekeeper said he couldn't have expressed it better himself. And then he told her what he'd done.

Vegetables and Salads

The Fall Chicken Supper

Counterclockwise from the chicken:
   Fried Chicken
   Fruit Coleslaw
   Baked Carrot Ring
   Kay's Layered Salad
   Turnips Revisited
   Rhubarb Relish and Mustard Pickles

Spring was one of the best parts of the Peace River country probably because winter was one of the worst. Spring meant mud and floods and aggravations of all sorts but it also meant incredibly sweet days, tiny wood violets you could barely see, brave red knobs of rhubarb pushing up through last year's debris.

Spring was also garden planting time and that meant, depending on your age, moving the stakes and strings or scattering the seeds into rows or following behind Dad to drop potatoes into the holes he made.

The garden was serious business and we knew it.

Immediately after planting came weeding. "You can go to the Bear Lake Sports if you weed ten rows first," or "You can finish your book after you finish the weeding."

Karen and Ken remember being paid 10 raisins a row in their time.

Then it meant picking and peeling and podding and canning.

It was an amazing despot.

Yet it brought some of the most exciting, certainly most delicious, slices of summer.

The first feed of peas was like a religious ceremony. We'd say to Mom, "Do you think they're ready? Can we have peas today?" And finally, she would pick just enough to add to carrots. She'd never go all out the first time and pick enough peas for peas alone.

But even that tease — a few peas in with the creamed carrots — was wonderful. There's nothing like fresh peas.

Then there would be the first feed of spinach or Swiss chard. Mom would cook it up plain, add butter, salt and pepper, and we'd swear we'd never tasted anything so good before. And, in fact, we hadn't for at least a year.

The garden climaxed with new potatoes. They were the very best, the highlight of the year . . . especially for Susan. Sometimes Mom would combine the best of two worlds and serve new potatoes with fresh peas. That combination is so good words fail me!

Sometimes Susan couldn't wait until the potatoes were ready to harvest, so she and Mom would cheat a bit and steal a few potatoes from the edge of a plant. That way, the whole plant was not dug up and remaining potatoes could grow to maturity.

Potatoes were a mainstay in our household. Dad never felt a meal was complete unless there were spuds, so Mom got in the habit of boiling a big batch for dinner and then frying up the leftovers for supper. That was our pattern interrupted only occasionally with potato salad or creamed new potatoes or scalloped potatoes. Usually scalloped potatoes were served in the spring when the potatoes down in the bin were getting soft and beginning to sprout.

It's interesting to look back now and see how much our menus were influenced by the seasons. We really couldn't have fresh vegetables all year round so when they did come into season, they were savoured and appreciated!

Not everyone had potatoes at every meal — a lesson that brother Jim learned at the tender age of five and a lesson he's never been allowed to forget.

We turned up at the schoolteachers' house late one afternoon — Mom, Dad and four kids. As was the custom, they automatically asked us to stay for supper.

They hadn't expected us, of course, but Mrs. McGrath simply stretched the beans and brown bread that she had been intending to serve her own family. All went well until Jim got his helping of beans, looked around and said, "What, no potatoes?"

He couldn't believe that anyone would serve beans without a generous heap of potatoes under the beans.

He still thinks that's the best combination but he's learned not to ask!

Interestingly, all those wonderful vegetables in our garden had to be cooked. Except for cabbage and lettuce, raw vegetables were not particularly popular in our household. Some kids were allowed to eat raw peas and pea pods but that practice never got by Mom. She just didn't think they were good for what ailed us. Now, when some of us grow pea pods just for the pods, she thinks we've lost the good sense she gave us.

Raw vegetables took on more respectability in the fall when we annually visited Early's Market Garden, for he was able to grow and sell the finest tomatoes and cucumbers in the country. Mind you, Mom hastened to pickle the cucumbers but we did get to eat the tomatoes as is — fresh and unbelievably good.

J. B. Early was a miracle worker in that famous garden of his. He coaxed out of that short growing season things like celery, peppers, cantaloup and watermelon. He also grew flowers to take your breath away; at one time he had 175 varieties of gladiolus. Visitors used to get a complimentary bouquet, and we always looked forward to our fall visit.

The vegetables and salads in the following section begin with the basics but quickly branch out into anything-but-basic. Because of our beginnings, we've all got a real affection for vegetables and we've even learned to love them raw! Join us! Read, eat and enjoy.

GARDEN FRESH NEW POTATOES AND NEW PEAS

Scrape enough new potatoes for the size of your family. Boil in as little water as possible until tender. Drain. Then add a few peas. Even if the pods aren't quite filled, the small new peas will be sweet and tender.

Add about half a cup (125 mL) sweet cream and let bubble through the potatoes and peas. Season with salt and pepper.

SCALLOPED POTATOES

5 or 6 medium potatoes, peeled and thinly sliced	5 or 6 medium potatoes, peeled and thinly sliced
2 tbsp. onion, chopped (or more if your family likes)	30 mL onion, chopped (or more if your family likes)
3 tbsp. flour	50 mL flour
grated parmesan cheese (optional)	grated parmesan cheese (optional)
2 tbsp. margarine	25 mL margarine
2 cups milk	500 mL milk

In a medium sized greased casserole, arrange one third of the potatoes on the bottom of the dish. Scatter with half the onion and half the flour, generous amounts of salt, pepper and parmesan cheese if desired. Repeat the layer and use the final one-third potatoes as a top layer. Sprinkle the top with salt, pepper, cheese and margarine. Pour in milk until it is just visible through the top layer of potatoes (but this depends on the density of the potato. If the potatoes begin to look a bit dry, add more milk half-way through the baking.)

Bake covered for half an hour at 350°F (180°C); then uncover for another half hour or until potatoes are tender when pierced with a fork.

HARVARD BEETS

3 cups sliced beets, (about 6 medium)	750 mL sliced beets, (about 6 medium)
⅓ cup vinegar	75 mL vinegar
¼ cup sugar	50 mL sugar
1 tbsp. cornstarch	15 mL cornstarch
½ tsp. salt	2 mL salt
½ cup water or beet liquid	125 mL water or beet liquid
1 tbsp. butter or margarine	15 mL butter or margarine

If using fresh beets, cook the beets, let cool slightly; peel and slice. If using canned, slice the beets and reserve the liquid.

In a two quart (2 L) saucepan, mix vinegar, sugar, cornstarch, salt and water or beet liquid. Stir over medium heat until smooth. Add butter or margarine. Add sliced beets and cook until beets are heated through. Stir occasionally.

POTATO SALAD WITH PEAS

8 medium sized potatoes	8 potatoes
1 cup sliced celery	250 mL sliced celery
3 green onions, tops and all	3 green onions, tops and all
½ cup mayonnaise	125 mL mayonnaise
⅓ cup sour cream	75 mL sour cream
1 tbsp. chopped fresh dill or	15 mL chopped fresh dill
1 tsp. dried dill weed	or 5 mL dried dill weed
1 tsp. salt	5 mL salt
pepper to taste	pepper to taste
1 cup frozen or fresh peas*	250 mL frozen or fresh peas*

Cook the potatoes until they're tender. While still warm, cut them into quarters and place in a large bowl. Add the sliced celery and chopped onion.

Combine the mayonnaise, sour cream, dill or dill weed, salt and pepper. Pour over the vegetables and toss gently. Add the peas and toss again.

Cover and let chill to blend flavours.

*You do not cook the peas. If frozen, make sure they're separated before adding to the potato mixture. If using fresh, pick the smallest and tenderest to use in the salad.

BAKED CARROT RING

2 lbs. carrots (8-10 medium)	1 kg carrots (8-10 medium)
1½ cups water	375 mL water
1½ tsp. salt	7 mL salt
2 eggs	2 eggs
1 cup milk	250 mL milk
1 cup soda biscuits, finely	250 mL soda biscuits, finely
crushed	crushed
¾ cup sharp cheddar cheese,	175 mL sharp cheddar cheese,
grated	grated
½ cup soft margarine	125 mL soft margarine
¼ cup minced onion	50 mL minced onion
¼ tsp. pepper	1 mL pepper
pinch cayenne pepper	pinch cayenne pepper

Cook clean carrots in the 1½ cups (375 mL) of water and salt; drain and mash.

Beat eggs with milk and add with the other ingredients to the mashed carrots. Mix well.

Place mixture in a greased ring pan and bake at 325°F (160°C) for 50-60 minutes.

Turn ring upside down on a platter. Serve with boiled green peas in centre dotted with butter and a sprig of parsley.

SINFUL MASHED POTATOES

6 medium potatoes
1 pkg. (3 oz.) cream cheese,
  softened
2 tbsp. butter
½ tsp. salt
¼ to ½ cup milk
pepper

6 medium potatoes
1 pkg. (125 g) cream cheese,
  softened
25 mL butter
2 mL salt
50 mL to 125 mL milk
pepper

Peel the potatoes, and boil in salted water until tender. Drain. Add the cream cheese*, butter and salt. Beat with an electric mixer until the mixture is thoroughly mashed and smooth. Add as much milk as necessary to bring to a creamy consistency. The amounts will vary with the kind of potato used, but as a rule, use less rather than more. You don't want sloppy mashed potatoes — just fluffy ones.

Place in a serving dish and sprinkle with freshly ground pepper.

*If the cream cheese has not been softened in advance, lay it on top of the potatoes for a few minutes until it loses some of its stiffness. Then add the butter and finish the mashing process.

BROCCOLI WITH HOLLANDAISE SAUCE

enough broccoli for the numbers
  expected
2 egg yolks
3 tbsp. lemon juice
½ cup butter

enough broccoli for the numbers
  expected
2 egg yolks
50 mL lemon juice
125 mL butter

Clean and cut up the broccoli. Make sure the stems are cut up so that they can cook as quickly as the flowerettes. Otherwise, let the stems cook a few minutes before adding the tops. However you do it, get a serving dish of steaming hot broccoli.

To make the hollandaise, place the egg yolks and lemon juice in a small saucepan. Using a wooden spoon, blend the two together. Cut the butter into thick slices and add about half the slices to the mixture in the saucepan.

Place the saucepan over low heat and stir rapidly with the wooden spoon until the butter is melted and the sauce thickened. Add the remaining butter, cook and stir constantly until the butter is melted and the sauce is thick and smooth.

Remove from heat, pour over the hot broccoli and enjoy.

Mom didn't fool around with sauces when she cooked the vegetables from our garden. They were always so fresh and so welcome that it would have been sacrilegious almost to hide the flavour and nutrition under heavy duty sauces. Instead, she put butter on almost everything, sometimes a light cream sauce on peas and carrots.

The modern version of putting butter on everything is hollandaise sauce. It's rich and adds the flavour that some of our store bought produce has lost in transit.

It's also easier than its name suggests!

RED CABBAGE FIT FOR A KING

3 tbsp. butter	50 mL butter
4 cups shredded red cabbage	1 L shredded red cabbage
1 cup apples, sliced	250 mL apples, sliced
3 tbsp. vinegar	50 mL vinegar
2 tbsp. brown sugar	30 mL brown sugar
1 tsp. salt	5 mL salt
½ tsp. prepared mustard	2 mL prepared mustard
pepper	pepper
½ cup sour cream	125 mL sour cream

Melt the butter in a saucepan or large fry pan. Add the cabbage and apple. Cook and stir until the butter coats the mixture and there are signs of softening. Don't let it get limp. Add the vinegar, sugar, salt, mustard and pepper. Cook another 2-5 minutes. This is not really intended to be cooked cabbage; it's more like the soft cabbage salad.

Finally, stir in the sour cream. Don't let the mixture boil after this addition. Just heat and serve.

CHEESE AND CABBAGE

1 small head of cabbage	1 small head of cabbage
4 tbsp. butter	50 mL butter
½ cup chopped onion	125 mL chopped onion
salt and pepper to taste	salt and pepper to taste
1 cup grated cheddar cheese	250 mL cheddar cheese

Slice cabbage about ¼ inch (8 mm) wide, chop slightly.

Melt butter in a heavy pot or fry pan. Saute the onion until soft and clear. Add the cabbage and salt and pepper to taste. Stir everything over low heat until the cabbage is softened and hot — about 5 minutes. Sprinkle cheese over cabbage, let it soften and then stir into the cabbage.

STUFFED TOMATOES

6 medium tomatoes	6 medium tomatoes
salt & pepper	salt & pepper
¾ cup coarse bread crumbs	175 mL coarse bread crumbs
4 tbsp. grated parmesan cheese	50 mL grated parmesan cheese
1 tbsp. chopped parsley	15 mL chopped parsley
¼ tsp. dried crushed basil	1 mL dried crushed basil
pinch dried oregano	pinch of dried oregano
pinch of garlic powder	pinch of garlic powder
3 tbsp. melted margarine	50 mL melted margarine

Cut top off tomatoes and scoop out seeds and centers. Sprinkle with salt and pepper.

Combine remaining ingredients; spoon into each tomato shell.

Place in greased baking dish. Bake at 350°F (180°C) for 20-25 minutes.

TURNIPS REVISITED

1 medium sized turnip	1 medium sized turnip
1 tbsp. butter	15 mL butter
½ cup brown sugar	125 mL brown sugar
1 tsp. cinnamon	5 mL cinnamon
4 apples, pared and sliced	4 apples, pared and sliced
⅓ cup flour	75 mL flour
⅓ cup brown sugar	75 mL brown sugar
2 tbsp. butter or margarine	25 mL butter or margarine

Peel the turnip; cook until tender. Drain. Mash with a masher or mixer and add the 1 tbsp. (15 mL) butter. Set aside.

Mix together the ½ cup (125 mL) brown sugar and cinnamon. Peel the apples; slice and toss with the sugar and cinnamon.

Mix the flour, the remaining brown sugar and the butter or margarine together until the mixture resembles coarse crumbs.

Now, grease a casserole dish. Put ⅓ the turnip mixture on the bottom. Layer with ½ the apple mixture. Repeat the layers ending up with a turnip layer. Over all, sprinkle the crumb mixture.

Bake in 350°F (180°C) oven for about an hour, until the apples are tender and the mixture is cooked through.

BAKED WINTER SQUASH

1 thick skinned squash*	1 thick skinned squash*
2 tbsp. honey or brown sugar	30 mL honey or brown sugar
2 tbsp. butter	30 mL butter

Cut the squash in half and remove the seeds. In the centre of each half, place 1 tbsp. (15 mL) honey or brown sugar and 1 tbsp. (15 mL) butter.

Wrap tightly in heavy aluminum foil and bake at 350°F. (180°C) for 1½-2 hours. Baking time depends on the size of the squash.

This is good baked along with the Thanksgiving or Christmas turkey.

*You can use any variety of the thick skinned squash . . . hubbard, acorn or buttercup.

DILLED ZUCCHINI

5 cups zucchini strips	1.25 L zucchini strips
¼ cup chopped onion	50 mL chopped onion
⅓ cup water	75 mL water
1 tsp. salt	5 mL salt
½ tsp. dried dill weed*	2 mL dried dill weed*
2 tbsp. butter or margarine	25 mL butter or margarine
2 tsp. sugar	10 mL sugar
1 tsp. lemon juice	5 mL lemon juice
2 tbsp. flour	30 mL flour
½ cup sour cream	125 mL sour cream

Cook together the zucchini, onion, water, salt and dill weed just until the zucchini is tender — maybe 5 minutes. You don't want the vegetables too limp. Do not drain. Add butter or margarine, sugar and lemon juice. Remove from heat.

Blend flour into the sour cream and add a bit of the hot cooking liquid to the sour cream mixture as well. Then put everything back in with the vegetables and cook until thickened.

Garnish with more dill if you have it.

*Use fresh dill if it's available.

ZUCCHINI CASSEROLE

2 medium sized zucchini	2 medium sized zucchini
2 medium sized onions	2 medium sized onions
3 tbsp. butter or margarine	50 mL butter or margarine
¼ cup water	50 mL water
3 tbsp. butter or margarine	50 mL butter or margarine
½ lb. fresh mushrooms	250 g fresh mushrooms
salt and pepper to taste	salt and pepper to taste
1 can tomato sauce, 14 oz.	1 can tomato sauce, 398 mL
1 cup grated parmesan cheese	250 mL grated parmesan cheese

Wash and slice the zucchini in thin crosswise slices. Likewise, slice the onion.

Melt 3 tbsp. (50 mL) butter or margarine in a saucepan and add the zucchini and onion. Stir the vegetables with the butter and then add water. Cover and let simmer for 3-4 minutes, just until the bite is out of the vegetables but not until they are limp.

In the meantime, in a medium sized fry pan, melt 3 tbsp. (50 mL) butter or margarine. Slice the mushrooms into the butter and fry lightly.

In a large greased baking dish, arrange one-half the zucchini and onion mixture. Use the liquid from the cooking process as well. Over that layer, sprinkle half the mushrooms. Salt and pepper to taste. Then pour over all one-half can of tomato sauce. Sprinkle finally with half the parmesan cheese.

Repeat the layer. Bake for 30-40 minutes, uncovered, in a 350°F (180°C) oven.

In the summer, you can substitute fresh tomatoes for the sauce. Just make a layer of sliced tomatoes.

Also, you can use stewed tomatoes or tomato juice instead of the tomato sauce, but cut out the cooking juices then or the casserole will be too runny.

DIANE'S VEGETABLE CASSEROLE

1 large potato	1 large potato
1 large tomato	1 large tomato
1 medium onion	1 medium onion
1 large zucchini	1 large zucchini
3 large carrots	3 large carrots
mushrooms	mushrooms
1 large potato (as last layer)	1 large potato (as last layer)
2½ cups grated cheddar cheese	625 mL grated cheddar cheese
salt, pepper and garlic powder	salt, pepper and garlic powder

Starting with potatoes, thinly slice all vegetables and arrange in layers in a 2 quart (2 L) casserole. Between each layer of vegetables season with spices. Between every second layer of vegetables spread grated cheese. Finish with a layer of potatoes. Sprinkle grated cheese on top.

Bake covered at 350°F (180°C) for approximately 1½ hours or until vegetables feel tender with fork.

NOTE: Fill casserole dish till heaping since it will shrink once cooked. You can delete or add any kind of vegetable.

A lot of imagination and work went into bridal showers in the early days. The hostess generally dreamt up a theme — something like a wishing well or a rainbow with a pot of gold at the other end or a ship about to sail off into happy-ever-after waters. That sort of thing.

There would often be a skit as the highlight of the program. A mock marriage was a favourite with various community women dressed up to represent the bride, groom, preacher and so on.

Lunch tended to be fancier than usual — little sandwiches, fancy cookies and more often than not . . . 24 hour salad.

Sometimes a collection of recipes would be put together for the bride-to-be and that always proved to be a most valuable and meaningful gift. Margie still relies on her handwritten collection of basic recipes.

Most of the recipes were sensible and terribly necessary. Sometimes, they weren't.

Like this one for bride's bread pudding . . .

"Crumble stale bread. Put in a bowl and cover with milk. Let soak a short time. Put out on the steps and call the dog."

24 HOUR SALAD

2 eggs, beaten
4 tbsp. vinegar
4 tbsp. sugar
2 tbsp. butter
1 cup whipping cream, whipped
2 bananas, diced
1 cup grapes, halved
2 oranges, peeled and cut*
14 oz. can fruit salad, drained
14 oz. can crushed pineapple, drained
2 cups miniature marshmallows

2 eggs, beaten
50 mL vinegar
50 mL sugar
25 mL butter
250 mL whipping cream, whipped
2 bananas, diced
250 mL grapes, halved
2 oranges, peeled and cut*
398 mL can fruit salad, drained
398 mL can crushed pineapple, drained
500 mL miniature marshmallows

In a double boiler, beat the eggs. Add vinegar and sugar, beating constantly until very thick and smooth. Add the butter and let cool. Fold in whipped cream, cut up fruits and marshmallows.

Set in the fridge for 24 hours before serving.

*You can substitute 1 can (10 oz. or 284 g) mandarin orange sections, drained.

24 HOUR SALAD UPDATED

1 can apricots, 14 oz.
1 can mandarin oranges, 14 oz.
1 can pineapple chunks, 14 oz.
1 cup shredded coconut*
1 cup sour cream
1 cup miniature marshmallows

1 can apricots, 398 mL
1 can mandarin oranges, 398 mL
1 can pineapple chunks, 398 mL
250 mL shredded coconut*
250 mL sour cream
250 mL miniature marshmallows

Drain the apricots and cut into chunks. Drain the mandarin orange sections and the pineapple. Add to the apricots. Add the coconut, sour cream and marshmallows. Cover and chill overnight.

Good served with pork, ham, or poultry.

Use the drained fruit juice in other recipes, or add it to the breakfast juice.

*The sweetened long grain coconut is particularly good in this recipe but other varieties work as well.

CARROT AND RAISIN SALAD

8 good sized carrots
½ cup raisins
½ cup mayonnaise
1 tbsp. lemon juice
salt and pepper to taste

8 good sized carrots
125 mL raisins
125 mL mayonnaise
15 mL lemon juice
salt and pepper to taste

Shred the carrots on a grater or use a food processor. Combine the finely shredded carrots with the raisins, mayonnaise and lemon juice. Toss lightly. Season with salt and pepper. (Use more mayonnaise if necessary).

FRUIT COLE SLAW

4 cups finely shredded cabbage	1 L finely shredded cabbage
salt and pepper	salt and pepper
¼ cup raisins	50 mL raisins
2 tbsp. green onion, chopped fine	25 mL green onion, chopped fine
2 oranges	2 oranges
2 medium bananas	2 medium bananas
½ cup mayonnaise	125 mL mayonnaise
½ cup commercial sour cream	125 mL commercial sour cream

Shred the cabbage and put into a large bowl. Sprinkle with salt and pepper to taste and add raisins and onions.

Peel oranges and cut into small pieces. Dice the bananas. Add both to the cabbage mixture. Then combine the mayonnaise and the sour cream; add to salad and toss.

Cover and chill well.

TANGY CARROT MOLD

3 oz. orange jelly powder	85 g orange jelly powder
¼ cup sugar	50 mL sugar
1½ cups boiling water	375 mL boiling water
8 oz. cream cheese, softened	250 g cream cheese, softened
½ cup orange juice	125 mL orange juice
½ tsp. grated lemon peel	2 mL grated lemon peel
2 tbsp. lemon juice	25 mL lemon juice
1 cup shredded carrots	250 mL shredded carrots
1 cup apple, chopped	250 mL apple, chopped

Dissolve orange jelly powder and sugar in boiling water. Add softened cream cheese and beat on low with electric mixer until smooth. (This tends to splatter so use a narrow bowl or big measuring cup.) Stir in the orange juice, lemon peel and lemon juice.

Chill until partially set. Add shredded carrots and apples. Pour into individual molds, or one big mold or a pretty glass bowl that can be put on the table as is. The salad is an attractive orange color, and it's particularly good with pork or ham.

TOMATO ASPIC

4 cups tomato juice	1 L tomato juice
6 oz. pkg. lemon or lime gelatine	170 g pkg. lemon or lime gelatine
⅓-½ cup cider vinegar	75-125 mL cider vinegar
pinch of cloves	pinch of cloves
1 cup celery and green onions	250 mL celery and green onions
mayonnaise to garnish	mayonnaise to garnish

Heat the tomato juice in a saucepan and add the gelatine. Stir well until the gelatine is thoroughly dissolved. Remove from heat and add the vinegar and cloves. Taste the aspic at this stage. If it's not quite tart enough, add a splash more cider vinegar. If it brings tears to your eyes, cut back the amount of vinegar next time. It should be snappy, however. Bland aspic is not too interesting.

Let cool. When the mixture begins to set, add the chopped celery and onions and pour into an attractive glass bowl to set. This can also be set in a mold, and un-molded at mealtime.

At serving time, garnish with mayonnaise so that everyone can get a bit as they help themselves to the salad.

COTTAGE CHEESE SALAD

3 oz. pkg. lime jelly powder	85 g pkg. lime jelly powder
¾ cup boiling water	175 mL boiling water
¾ cup crushed pineapple, drained	175 mL crushed pineapple
¾ cup pineapple juice*	175 mL pineapple juice*
1 cup creamed cottage cheese	250 mL creamed cottage cheese
⅓ cup salad dressing or mayonnaise	75 mL salad dressing or mayonnaise

Dissolve the jelly powder in the boiling water. Add crushed pineapple and pineapple juice. Chill until slightly thickened.

Combine the cottage cheese and salad dressing or mayonnaise and add to the gelatine mixture. Pour into a mold and chill.

Serve as is, or unmold and garnish with whatever looks good.

If using homemade cottage cheese, add ¼ cup (50 mL) of cream to 1 cup (250 mL) cottage cheese and proceed as above.

*Use the juice drained from the crushed pineapple.

COTTAGE CHEESE WALDORF SALAD

4 medium sized apples, diced	4 medium sized apples, diced
½ cup golden raisins	125 mL golden raisins
½ cup chopped walnuts	125 mL walnuts
1 tbsp. sugar	15 mL sugar
1 tbsp. lemon juice	15 mL lemon juice
½ cup cottage cheese	125 mL cottage cheese
½ cup sour cream	125 mL sour cream

Combine apples, raisins and walnuts. Sprinkle with sugar and lemon juice; toss lightly.

Blend cottage cheese and sour cream and pour over apple mixture. Again, toss lightly.

CUCUMBERS IN SOUR CREAM

1 cucumber	1 cucumber
1 small onion	1 small onion
2 tsp. salt	10 mL salt
½ cup sour cream	125 mL sour cream
1 tsp. vinegar	5 mL vinegar
1 tsp. sugar	5 mL sugar
pepper	pepper

If the cucumber is waxed, peel it. Otherwise, just wash it and slice as is. You can score the skin by running the tines of a fork down the length of the cucumber. It looks a bit fancier that way.

Anyway, slice the cucumber as thinly as possible. Sprinkle with 1 tsp. salt (5 mL). Slosh the mixture around a bit so that all of the cucumber meets some of the salt.

Also, slice the onion as thinly as possible and put in another small bowl. Sprinkle with the remaining 1 tsp. (5 mL) salt.

Let both stand for about 15 minutes. Then drain the juice from each, making sure as much liquid as possible is removed. The cucumbers should be almost limp.

Make a dressing by mixing together the sour cream, vinegar, sugar and pepper. Combine the cucumbers and onions, pour the dressing over and serve.

BEAN SALAD

1 can kidney beans (14 oz.)	1 can kidney beans (398 mL)
1 can yellow wax beans (14 oz.)	1 can yellow wax beans (398 mL)
1 can green beans (14 oz.)	1 can green beans (398 mL)
1 can lima beans (14 oz.)*	1 can lima beans (398 mL)*
1-2 green peppers, chopped	1-2 green peppers, chopped
1 onion, sliced in rings	1 onion, sliced in rings
½ cup vinegar	125 mL vinegar
½ cup sugar	125 mL sugar
½ cup oil	125 mL oil
½ tsp. celery seed	2 mL celery seed
salt and pepper to taste	salt and pepper to taste

Drain liquid off the four cans of beans. In a large bowl, combine the beans, chopped green pepper and onion rings.

Mix the vinegar, sugar, oil, celery seed and salt and pepper. Pour over the beans and mix well. Refrigerate, covered, for several hours or overnight. Stir once in awhile.

This salad keeps for 4-5 days in the fridge.

*You could use garbanzo beans as well.

MARINATED CUCUMBERS

1 medium cucumber	1 medium cucumber
1 small onion	1 small onion
½ cup vinegar	125 mL vinegar
½ cup water*	125 mL water*
2 tbsp. sugar	30 mL sugar
¼ tsp. salt	1 mL salt

Thinly slice the cucumber and onion.

Mix together the vinegar, water, sugar and salt and pour over the vegetables. Refrigerate at least 2 hours before serving.

*If you like a very tart taste, leave out the water and use vinegar only. The cucumbers will bite back, and many people like them that way.

KAY'S LAYERED SALAD

1 head iceberg lettuce	1 head iceberg lettuce
8-10 green onions	8-10 green onions
1 can water chestnuts (8 oz.)	1 can water chestnuts (227 mL)
½ green pepper	½ green pepper
3 stalks celery	3 stalks celery
1 pkg. frozen peas (2 cups)	1 pkg. frozen peas (500 mL)
2 cups mayonnaise	500 mL mayonnaise
2 tsp. sugar	10 mL sugar
½ cup grated parmesan	125 mL grated parmesan
1 tsp. salt	5 mL salt
healthy dash of ground pepper	healthy dash of ground pepper
¼ tsp. garlic powder	1 mL garlic powder
¾ lb. bacon, fried and chopped	375 g bacon, fried and chopped
3 hard boiled eggs	3 hard boiled eggs
2 tomatoes	2 tomatoes

The most important ingredient for this very good salad is a large straight sided glass bowl because the vegetables are arranged in layers. Half the fun in the eating of this salad is in the seeing beforehand!

In the glass bowl, arrange the crisped cut up lettuce first. That forms the bottom layer. Then put the rest of the ingredients in layers on top of the lettuce, in the order given above. Don't add the tomatoes until serving time, but put everything else in the bowl. Spread each layer evenly over the layer below.

Chill for at least 4 hours or overnight. Keep the salad covered in the fridge — it has a potent aroma!

Incidentally, do not cook the peas. They thaw in the chilling process and taste like fresh when the salad is served.

To serve, garnish with the tomatoes. Explain to guests that they should try to get some of each layer, or better yet, serve it to guests, making sure everyone gets some of each layer.

CARROT SALAD

1½ lbs. carrots (8-10 medium)	750 g carrots (8-10 medium)
1 medium onion, thinly sliced	1 medium onion, thinly sliced
1 medium green pepper, in strips	1 medium green pepper, in strips
½ can tomato soup (10 oz. size)	½ can tomato soup (284 g size)
½ cup sugar	125 mL sugar
½ cup oil	125 mL oil
⅓ cup vinegar	75 mL vinegar
½ tsp. salt	2 mL salt
½ tsp. dry mustard	2 mL dry mustard
¼ tsp. pepper	1 mL pepper

Clean carrots, peel and slice. Cook approximately 5-8 minutes. They should be a bit crunchy still. Drain and add the sliced onion and green pepper.

Mix the tomato soup, sugar, oil, vinegar, salt, dry mustard and pepper in a saucepan and heat, stirring constantly, until sugar is dissolved. Cool slightly and then pour over carrots. Refrigerate until ready to serve.

Will keep 2-3 weeks.

SPINACH SALAD

fresh spinach	fresh spinach
½ lb. mushrooms, sliced	250 g mushrooms, sliced
½ lb. bacon, fried and crumbled	250 g bacon, fried and crumbled
3 eggs, hardboiled and diced	3 eggs, hardboiled, diced
2 tomatoes, quartered	2 tomatoes, quartered

For six people, buy two bunches of fresh spinach (or with any luck, pick enough fresh spinach to fill a medium sized bowl). Clean the leaves. With store bought spinach, you almost have to clean each leaf individually. With home grown, you may be able to rinse it carefully in bunches. Anyway, clean it and let drain on absorbent towelling. Wrap in the towelling and keep in crisper until time to put the salad together.

In the meantime, clean the mushrooms. Try not to get them too wet in the cleaning process. If they're quite clean, just wipe them off. If not, wash but let drain thoroughly.

Cut up the bacon and fry until crisp. Wrap in absorbent paper until needed.

Boil the eggs, let cool and peel.

To assemble the salad, tear up the spinach leaves into the bottom of a big salad bowl. Over the spinach, place the sliced mushrooms and fried bacon. Dice the hardboiled eggs and sprinkle on top. Lastly, arrange the quartered tomatoes around the outside of the bowl. Serve with a creamy dressing (page 98).

SHEILA'S CREAMY DRESSING

½ cup mayonnaise	125 mL mayonnaise
½ cup sour cream or yogurt	125 mL sour cream or yogurt
2 tbsp. green onion tops, diced	30 mL green onion tops, diced
2 tbsp. minced parsley*	30 mL minced parsley*
1½ tbsp. vinegar	20 mL vinegar
1½ tbsp. lemon juice	20 mL lemon juice
1 clove garlic, minced**	1 clove garlic, minced**

Combine the ingredients and let stand for half an hour or so to let the flavours blend.

For a spinach salad, serve in a separate bowl so that people can select the amount they prefer for their salad. For a chip dip, put into a bowl and serve with chips, etc. For a vegetable tray, serve separately as well.

*The parsley is best fresh but dried parsley will do in a pinch.
**Garlic powder may be substituted for fresh garlic. Use about ½ tsp. (2 mL).

NO HOLDS BARRED GARLIC DRESSING

1 cup olive or good light oil	250 mL olive or good light oil
¾ cup light cream	175 mL light cream
¼ cup cider vinegar	50 mL cider vinegar
2 eggs	2 eggs
1 clove garlic, crushed	1 clove garlic, crushed
1 tsp. dry mustard	5 mL dry mustard
dash of salt and pepper	dash of salt and pepper

Combine all the ingredients in a blender and process for about 3 minutes. Pour into a glass jar with a screw top and refrigerate until needed. Shake well before using.

Will keep for several weeks.

Also, it's easy to halve this recipe if you're having a small gathering.

BLUE CHEESE DRESSING

⅛ lb. blue cheese	63 g blue cheese
1 cup sour cream	250 mL sour cream
1 cup mayonnaise	250 mL mayonnaise
1 clove garlic, minced	1 clove garlic, minced
1 tbsp. lemon juice	15 mL lemon juice
¼ cup buttermilk or yogurt	50 mL buttermilk or yogurt
salt and pepper to taste	salt and pepper to taste

Chop the blue cheese into small chunks and stir in the rest of the ingredients. Let stand to blend flavours for a few minutes before serving.

Can be stored in the fridge for several weeks.

Desserts

Desserts Take the Cake

Strawberry Shortcake

Summer in the Peace River country yielded up such riches — among them . . . wild berries.

Mom has always loved to make something out of nothing so to get pail after pail of big juicy raspberries, for example, was like winning a lottery for her or discovering oil!

Strawberries were the first on the scene — small, incredibly sweet berries hidden under grass and leaves. One moment you'd just be standing around — waiting for the school bus perhaps — and then out of the corner of your eye you'd see a flash of red. And sure enough, once you bent down and adjusted your eyes, there would be strawberries all over the place — by the side of the road, in the ditch, in the field beyond. And you ate them, of course, right there and then.

Such bounty.

Mom would hear of the patch and come back to pick systematically. Or she'd be out with Dad looking at crops or fixing fences and they'd find a patch. Off would come Dad's hat or they'd scrounge an old can from the back of the truck and they'd stop to pick strawberries.

Strawberries were always an unexpected bonus. You couldn't depend on them. They were just there sometimes and you were invited to partake.

Occasionally Mom would persevere and get a bowlful, enough for some very precious jam or a strawberry shortcake. But for me, they were best as found, like some sort of secret offering.

Raspberries came next and I wasn't nearly so enthusiastic. As far as I was concerned, picking raspberries was a hot, prickly, mosquito ridden, bear haunted activity. Fortunately for the dinner table, Mom loved it.

In the early days, there were lots of patches in the Beaton Creek and Whitemud Valleys, and neighbors used to share their special spots . . . within limits!

Mom would tell a neighbour lady that there were lots of raspberries down in the flat, but since the flat wandered for miles along the creek, her description didn't exactly narrow down the location.

But they were very specific in telling one another how many quarts they had canned.

Saskatoon picking was much more fun for us kids mainly because it generally involved a trip for Berwyn and a visit with the cousins. The best saskatoons were found along the Peace River valley and since Uncle Albert eventually had land in that area, that's where we would head.

It was always an adventure. Generally we got stuck on a side hill somewhere, with Mom absolutely convinced we were all going to end up in the river. Sometimes we lost a cousin or two, and always we had to move frequently, looking for that one last perfect patch.

It was always a lovely lark, and somehow Mom managed to get a few berries in between all the other diversions.

Saskatoons are beautiful to behold — like so many small blue grapes hanging on gracefully bent branches. They're not that wonderful out of hand but they're very good in sauces, pies, jams and puddings. They're also very good in combinations with other fruits.

Saskatoons are getting harder and harder to find but the cousins can still occasionally find a spot that hasn't been sprayed or cleared away. Raspberries, alas, have more or less disappeared.

After saskatoons came high bush cranberries. We didn't have to hunt them out — they signalled their readiness by a rotten sweet smell that was unmistakable. Jim or Ken would come home from a day in the fields and say . . . "There are high bush cranberries on the west of Carl's old field" or, "across the gully at Agner's" and so on. They never had to get off the tractor to make this diagnosis — they just followed their noses.

In spite of the smell, high bush cranberries make very tasty and beautiful jelly — a clear ruby colored potion with a bite and sass that says more.

Occasionally, some of the women would find blueberries in the early days too. Now that was an exercise in frustration — tiny little berries hidden in moss and leaves — but again, Mom would get some if she heard of them. They were, it must be admitted, incredibly tasty.

Finally, there would be low bush cranberries, a smaller version of the domestic cranberries that are sold now in supermarkets at Thanksgiving and Christmastime. They could be found in muskegs, in among moss and twigs and leaves and fallen trees. Again, it was a real exercise in perseverance to pick the tiny berries but it too was well rewarded. They had a tart/sweet taste that was incomparable in pie, for example. Mom's low bush cranberry pie took first prize at the exhibition for years.

The low bush cranberry is more or less extinct now too what with muskegs having been cleared for fields and roads. Progress means you win some and you lose some. It never fails!

And all summer long, there was rhubarb. It wasn't a wild berry although it grew like wildfire around most homes. Dad had a way with rhubarb and in the very early days, neighbours used to come to him for roots and advice. But once established, it was the first thing to come up in the spring and it hung around after the frosts in the fall. So it was a standby if ever there was one!

When the stalks were still pretty small, Mom would make a rhubarb cobbler. That way she could use just a bit of fruit and cover it with a lot of cake topping. Then as the stalks got bigger, she'd make rhubarb crisp and rhubarb pie and rhubarb jam and rhubarb juice and rhubarb pickles and rhubarb ice cream.

You wouldn't believe what we did with rhubarb!

One of the oldtimers used to dry it to take along with him on the trapline the following winter.

It was the one garden commodity that Mom let us waste — just a bit! Jim used to chase me around the yard with the big seed stalks. We used the big leaves for hats and the seeds for mud pie decorations. We hid in it when playing hide and seek.

It's no wonder the five of us plant rhubarb everywhere we land . . . and no wonder that we have more rhubarb desserts than any other kind.

There are other kinds, however, if you're not as crazy about rhubarb as we are! Read, eat and enjoy.

OLD FASHIONED BREAD PUDDING

3 cups bread crumbs	750 mL bread crumbs
2 cups milk	500 mL milk
¼ cup butter	50 mL butter
½ cup sugar	125 mL sugar
¼ tsp. salt	1 mL salt
1 tsp. cinnamon or nutmeg	5 mL cinnamon or nutmeg
2 eggs, slightly beaten	2 eggs, slightly beaten
½ cup raisins	125 mL raisins

Place bread crumbs in 1½ qt. (1.5 L) greased baking dish. If you prefer a firmer pudding, use an extra cup of bread crumbs.

Scald milk with butter; add sugar, salt and spices and mix well. Pour over the bread crumb mixture. Beat eggs slightly and add to the mixture. Sprinkle with raisins.

Place baking dish in a pan of hot water 1" (2.5 cm) deep. Bake 40-45 minutes in 350°F (180°C) oven. When it's done, a silver knife inserted into the centre will come out clean.

Serve warm with cream.

COCOA BREAD PUDDING

Use 2 tbsp. (30 mL) cocoa instead of spices. Mix it well with the sugar and salt, take a bit of the hot milk and stir it together to make sure lumps are worked out. Then put it back into the bread and milk mixture.

If Friday was baking day, then Thursday was bread pudding day!

Bread baked once a week tended to get pretty dry by the end of its weekly run, so homemakers used up the crusts and the stale bits in bread puddings.

Eventually, bread pudding became so popular that homemakers made it all week round. But it's still one of the best examples of the old adage:

Use it up
Wear it out
Make it do
Or do without.

MARIAN'S RICE PUDDING

⅔ cup long grain rice	150 mL long grain rice
3 cups milk	750 mL milk
½ cup raisins	125 mL raisins
2 eggs	2 eggs
½ cup sugar	125 mL sugar
1 tsp. vanilla	5 mL vanilla
½ tsp. nutmeg	2 mL nutmeg
½ cup milk	125 mL milk

Combine the rice, 3 cups (750 mL) milk and raisins in a well buttered dish and bake in 350°F (180°C) oven until the rice is cooked. It may take 30-45 minutes. If the combination gets dry, add more milk as needed.

Beat the eggs and add sugar, vanilla, nutmeg and ½ cup (125 mL) milk. Stir into the hot rice mixture, making sure it's mixed in well. Continue baking at the same temperature until the custard is set, another 30-45 minutes. If you like a creamy rice pudding, you may want to add more milk than is indicated. Use your judgment.

Many early homesteaders farmed in the summer and trapped in the winter. Sometimes, in fact, the winter's trapline supported the summer's farming because wild animals were abundant in the early days and prices for fur were pretty good.

But life on the trapline was pretty lonesome — no company, no newspapers, no nothing. So trappers devised various schemes to make time pass — like trapper's ice cream.

According to Harry Beebe who used to visit with the returning trappers, making the so-called ice cream would take a whole evening. You'd put the simple ingredients together in a bowl and then set it out in a snowbank. Every half hour or so, you dashed out into the cold to stir the freezing mixture until it was completely frozen and ready to eat.

TRAPPER's ICE CREAM

1 can evaporated milk	454 g evaporated milk
1 tsp. vanilla	5 mL vanilla
½ cup grapenut cereal	125 mL grapenut cereal

Mix together milk, vanilla and cereal in a mixing bowl; set bowl outside in the snowbank. Run outside every once in awhile to stir until mixture freezes.

BAKED CUSTARD

2 eggs	2 eggs
¼ cup sugar	50 mL sugar
½ tsp. salt	2 mL salt
1 tsp. vanilla or almond extract	5 mL vanilla or almond extract
2 cups milk, scalded	500 mL milk, scalded
nutmeg to taste	nutmeg to taste

Beat eggs slightly. Add sugar, salt and flavouring. Slowly pour into this the scalded milk, and stir until sugar is dissolved. Pour into greased individual molds or casserole. Shake nutmeg over top.

Set in pan of hot water and bake in a 350ºF (180ºC) oven for about 1 hour. To test if done, insert knife in centre of custard, and if the blade is clean when withdrawn the custard is done.

Serve hot or cold with a topping of maple syrup, jam or your favourite fresh fruit slices. Try adding ½ cup (125 mL) coconut to egg mixture for a pleasant variation.

During war years when sugar was rationed, the custard was a favourite recipe because it took very little sugar. Some people served it as a pudding; others made it into pie. Custard pie was Albert Banks' all time favourite, even when fresh berries were available.

The community history book tells a good story about Mr. and Mrs. Banks who played such an important part in the development of the community. It seems that they eloped before Mrs. Banks was of the proper age. But they were able to honestly swear that she was "over" 18 because they had written the number 18 on a piece of paper and put it in her shoe.

Thus she was — technically — "over" 18.

With that kind of creativity and imagination, no wonder they were such successful homesteaders.

RHUBARB CRISP

4 cups cut up rhubarb	1 L cut up rhubarb
1 cup sugar	250 mL sugar
¼ cup flour	50 mL flour
½ tsp. cinnamon	2 mL cinnamon
1 cup flour	250 mL flour
½ cup rolled oats	125 mL rolled oats
1 cup brown sugar	250 mL brown sugar
½ cup butter or margarine	125 mL butter or margarine

Combine rhubarb, 1 cup (250 mL) sugar, ¼ cup (50 mL) flour and cinnamon and put into an 8 x 8" (2 L) baking dish or casserole.

Combine flour, rolled oats, brown sugar and cut in the butter or margarine to form crumbs. Sprinkle over the rhubarb.

Bake at 350ºF (180ºC) for about 40 minutes or until the rhubarb is tender and juicy. Serve warm with various versions of pouring cream, whipped cream or ice cream.

LEMON SPONGE PUDDING

¾ cup sugar	175 mL sugar
2 tbsp. soft butter	25 mL soft butter
3 egg yolks	3 egg yolks
2 tsp. grated lemon rind	10 mL grated lemon rind
¼ cup flour	50 mL flour
¼ tsp. salt	1 mL salt
1 cup milk	250 mL milk
¼ cup lemon juice	50 mL lemon juice
3 egg whites	3 egg whites

Cream sugar, butter, egg yolks and lemon rind thoroughly. Combine the flour and salt and add to the creamed mixture alternately with the milk and lemon juice.

Beat egg whites until stiff but not dry. Fold into batter. Pour mixture into greased 1½ qt. (1½ L) casserole. Place in the oven in a pan of hot water 1" (2.5 cm) deep.

Bake at 350°F (180°C) for about an hour or until set.

Serve hot or cold, with or without whipped cream.

This is the kind of pudding that forms a fluffy cake top with a lemon sauce beneath. Delicious!

AUNT MABLE'S FUDGE PUDDING

1 cup flour	250 mL flour
2 tsp. baking powder	10 mL baking powder
¾ cup sugar	175 mL sugar
½ tsp. salt	2 mL salt
3 tbsp. cocoa	50 mL cocoa
½ cup milk	125 mL milk
2 tbsp. melted shortening	25 mL melted shortening
¼ cup chopped walnuts, optional	50 mL chopped walnuts, optional
¾ cup brown sugar	175 mL brown sugar
½ cup cocoa	125 mL cocoa
2 cups boiling water	500 mL boiling water

Mix together first five ingredients. Combine the milk and melted shortening and mix into the dry ingredients. Add walnuts, if desired. Batter will be stiff.

Pour into a greased baking dish — an 8 x 8" pan (2 L) or a suitable casserole.

Combine the brown sugar and cocoa and sprinkle over the first batter. Finally, pour the boiling water over everything.* It's a good idea to pour the water over the batter when it's already in the oven. That way you won't have to carry a full dish across a crowded room!

Bake in a 350°F (180°C) for 40 minutes or so, or until the batter rises to the top and is baked through.

Serve hot as is, or with whipped cream or ice cream.

*You could mix the brown sugar, cocoa and boiling water together and then pour over the batter. Either method seems to work fine.

---

*B*oth *Lemon Sponge Pudding* and *Hot Fudge Pudding* *are self saucing puddings and generally served hot.*

They were particularly welcome as winter desserts when the cold winds whistled around the corners of the house and the temperatures steadfastly dropped. Then they spoke somehow of comfort and warmth, a shelter from the storm.

They were also quick and economical.

APPLE BETTY

6 apples	6 apples
¼ cup sugar	50 mL sugar
½ tsp. nutmeg	2 mL nutmeg
½ tsp. cinnamon	2 mL cinnamon
2 tbsp. lemon juice	25 mL lemon juice
½ cup flour	125 mL flour
¾ cup brown sugar	175 mL brown sugar
¼ tsp. salt	1 mL salt
¼ cup butter or margarine	50 mL butter or margarine

Peel, core and slice the apples. Mix the sugar and spices together and toss with the apples. Put into a greased casserole or baking dish. Sprinkle with lemon juice.

Mix the flour, brown sugar and salt together. Cut in the butter or margarine until the mixture resembles fine crumbs. Put the crumbs on top of the apple mixture and bake at 350°F (180°C) for 40 minutes or thereabouts. Check to see that the fruit is tender and juicy before removing from the oven.

Serve hot or cold with whipped cream or ice cream.

This Betty recipe forms into a crunchy crust better than many others. It works just as well on rhubarb, wild berries, canned fruit. Adjust the sugar and the baking time for each fruit used. Also, try ½ cup (125 mL) raisins with the fruit.

STRAWBERRY SHORTCAKE

2 cups flour	500 mL flour
2 tbsp. sugar	30 mL sugar
3 tsp. baking powder	15 mL baking powder
dash of salt	dash of salt
½ cup butter or margarine	125 mL butter or margarine
⅔ cup cereal cream	150 mL cereal cream
1 egg	1 egg
butter for spreading	butter for spreading
3-4 cups sliced strawberries*	750 mL-1L sliced strawberries*
1 cup whipping cream, whipped	250 mL whipping cream, whipped

In medium bowl, combine flour, sugar, baking powder and salt. Cut in butter or margarine until mixture resembles coarse crumbs.

In a smaller bowl or measuring cup, beat together the cereal cream and the egg, and add the two to the dry ingredients. Spread evenly in a greased round cake pan or greased 8 x 8" (2 L) baking pan or make individual biscuits. Bake at 450°F (230°C) for about 15 minutes or until golden brown. The biscuits will take less time, perhaps 10-12 minutes. Remove from pan and cool on wire rack for about 5 minutes.

For a round cake, cut the shortcake horizontally into two layers. Lift top off carefully. Butter the bottom layer, spoon on half the berries and whipped cream. Put the top layer back on and cover with remaining berries and cream.

Makes a stunning dessert, both from a taste perspective and sight perspective.

*Sweeten the berries to taste.

UPSIDE DOWN APPLE CAKE

3 tbsp. butter	50 mL butter
¾ cup brown sugar	175 mL brown sugar
5 apples, peeled and sliced	5 apples, peeled and sliced
3 tbsp. lemon juice	50 mL lemon juice
1 egg	1 egg
1 cup white sugar	250 mL white sugar
1 cup whipping cream	250 mL whipping cream
1 tsp. vanilla	5 mL vanilla
2 cups flour	500 mL flour
2 tsp. baking powder	10 mL baking powder

Melt the butter in a round baking dish and mix in the brown sugar. Arrange the apple slices over top and sprinkle with lemon juice.

In another bowl, beat the egg, add the sugar, whipping cream and vanilla. Combine the flour and baking powder and add to the egg mixture. Pour over the apples.

Bake at 350°F (180°C) for 30 minutes or until toothpick inserted in the centre of the cake comes out clean.

Let cool for 10 minutes in the pan; then invert and turn out onto a serving dish.

Serve warm with ice cream or whipped cream.

You can do exactly the same thing with pineapple. Just substitute pineapple rings for the apples, and you'll have a very tasty pineapple upside down cake.

RHUBARB COBBLER

3-4 cups chopped rhubarb	750 mL to 1 L chopped rhubarb
1 cup sugar	250 mL sugar
3 oz. box strawberry gelatin	85 g strawberry gelatin
1½ cups flour	375 mL flour
2 tsp. baking powder	10 mL baking powder
½ tsp. salt	2 mL salt
½ cup butter or margarine	125 mL butter or margarine
1 cup sugar	250 mL sugar
1 egg	1 egg
¾ cup milk	175 mL milk
1 tsp. vanilla	5 mL vanilla
1 tsp. cinnamon	5 mL cinnamon
1 tbsp. sugar	15 mL sugar

Wash and cut rhubarb into small pieces. Mix with the 1 cup (250 mL) sugar and gelatin.

Sift flour, baking powder and salt together.

Cream butter or margarine and 1 cup (250 mL) sugar. Beat in egg. Add dry ingredients alternately with milk and vanilla. Blend until batter is smooth.

In a well greased baking dish, layer the fruit mixture on the bottom. Spread the batter over the fruit.

Mix the cinnamon with the 1 tbsp. (15 mL) sugar and sprinkle over the top. Bake at 350°F (180°C) for 45-50 minutes or until the rhubarb is bubbly and soft.

Cut in squares and serve warm with ice cream, whipped cream or pouring cream.

This works well with other fresh fruits like saskatoons, plums, cherries, even apples. Vary the gelatin to suit the fruit.

CREAM PUFFS

½ cup butter	125 mL butter
1 cup boiling water	250 mL boiling water
1 cup flour	250 mL flour
¼ tsp. salt	1 mL salt
4 eggs	4 eggs

Melt butter in boiling water. Add flour and salt all at once; stir vigorously. Cook, stirring constantly, until mixture forms a ball that doesn't separate. Remove from heat. Add eggs one at a time, beating vigorously after each until the batter is smooth.

Drop dough by heaping tablespoons 3" (8 cm) apart on greased cookie sheet. Bake in 450°F (230°C) oven for 15 minutes; then in 325°F (160°C) oven for 25 minutes. Remove from oven; split. Turn oven off and put cream puffs back in oven to dry out — about 20 minutes. Cool on racks.

Just before serving, fill centres with sweetened whipped cream, or a custard filling.

Nowadays cream puffs are brought out for special occasions only but homestead housewives used them fairly frequently.

Cream puffs, after all, require only those things that every farm had in abundance — cream, butter and eggs.

Susan particularly remembers Mrs. Julia Macas' cream puffs. She would make a big batch and then say. . . Eat, eat, eat . . . to her company. Susan was only too glad to oblige.

HOMEMADE ICE CREAM

4 eggs	4 eggs
2 cups sugar	500 mL sugar
5 cups milk	1.25 L milk
4 cups heavy cream	1 L heavy cream
2 tbsp. vanilla	30 mL vanilla
½ tsp. salt	2 mL salt

In a large bowl, beat the eggs and add the sugar gradually, beating until mixture is stiff. Add remaining ingredients and mix thoroughly. Pour into gallon freezer can and turn the crank until done, or plug in the cord. Follow the instructions, in other words, for whatever kind of ice cream maker you have.

If you want a lighter ice cream, increase the percentage of milk and correspondingly decrease the cream. You'll get an ice milk product that's easier on the waistline.

Also, you can add whatever fruits strike your fancy as you make this basic ice cream. If the fruits are presweetened (as with frozen raspberries or strawberries) cut down on the amount of sugar. If the fruits have a tart edge, add a bit of sugar (as with fresh raspberries or blueberries.) Taste the mixture before it goes into the ice cream can, and if it needs sugar, add some. Be sure to stir the mixture well to dissolve the sugar before it goes into the ice cream can. It will not get worked in completely once it's in the freezing process so do that first.

Homemade ice cream was an enormous treat — not because of the cream but because of the ice. Cream was plentiful; ice was not.

Some people had ice houses so homemade ice cream would turn up occasionally at picnics or ballgames. But for those of us without ice or refrigeration, it was a rare treat.

Eventually, Uncle Albert got himself an ice supply and we would look forward to having ice cream when we visited the cousins. Taking our turns at the crank was all part of the fun.

It is fitting that the recipes for homemade ice cream and yogurt ice cream come from one of the cousins who carried on the tradition . . . our cousin Rita.

YOGURT ICE CREAM

10-12 cups yogurt
fruit
sugar to taste
1 pkg. unflavoured gelatin
¼ cup water

2.5L-3L yogurt
fruit
sugar to taste
1 pkg. unflavoured gelatin
50 mL water

Use unflavoured yogurt, whether of the homemade or store bought variety.

Use fresh, frozen or canned fruit. If the fruit is already sweetened, you may not have to add further sugar. One of the attractions of yogurt ice cream is its slightly tart flavour so you don't want to load it down with sugar. If, however, you're using a tart unsweetened fruit, you may need to add sugar. Taste the combination as you go along. If it tastes good before it goes through the ice cream process, it will taste even better after it's been processed.

Anyway, add the fruit to the yogurt.

Dissolve the gelatin in the cold water. Stir it into the yogurt mixture just before pouring into the freezer can.

Follow instructions that come with your particular ice cream maker.

Rita made yogurt ice cream with canned apricots once. She just chopped up the fruit and added it, juice and all, to homemade yogurt. It was a very refreshing combination.

RHUBARB TRIFLE

4 cups sliced rhubarb	1 L sliced rhubarb
¾ cup sugar	175 mL sugar
1 tbsp. cornstarch	15 mL cornstarch
½ cup water	125 mL water
few drops red food colouring	few drops red food colouring
⅓ cup sugar	75 mL sugar
2 tbsp. cornstarch	30 mL cornstarch
2 cups milk	500 mL milk
2 egg yolks, beaten	2 egg yolks, beaten
2 tbsp. butter or margarine	25 mL butter or margarine
2 tsp. vanilla	10 mL vanilla
sponge cake or meringues	sponge cake or meringues
sherry or fruit juice	sherry or fruit juice

Clean and cut rhubarb into small pieces, enough to make 4 cups (1 L). Set aside.

In a medium sized pot, combine the sugar, cornstarch, and water. Heat to boiling and add rhubarb. Simmer about 10 minutes or until rhubarb is tender and slightly transparent. Stir in the red food colouring. Cool completely.

In another saucepan, blend the ⅓ cup sugar (75 mL) and 2 tbsp. cornstarch (30 mL). Combine the milk and egg yolks and beat slightly. Add to sugar mixture and cook over medium heat, stirring constantly, until mixture thickens and boils. Boil and stir 1 minute. Remove from heat and add the butter or margarine and the vanilla. Cool completely.

In an attractive glass bowl, arrange slices of sponge cake (or left over plain white cake). You may also use 4-5 purchased meringues . . . crumble them up and arrange on the bottom of the bowl.

Sprinkle the cake or the meringue crumbs with sweet sherry or fruit juice. Spoon about ⅓ of the custard mixture over the cake or the meringues. Spoon over that ½ the rhubarb. Repeat layers — next a custard, then rhubarb and finally custard. Sprinkle with more meringue crumbs, if using meringues. Otherwise, chill for several hours.

Serve with whipped cream.

LEMON CRUNCH

½ cup sugar	125 mL sugar
2½ tbsp. cornstarch	35 mL cornstarch
¼ tsp. salt	1 mL salt
1⅓ cups milk	325 mL milk
1 egg, beaten	1 egg, beaten
¼ cup lemon juice	50 mL lemon juice
grated peel of one lemon	grated peel of one lemon
1 tbsp. butter	15 mL butter
½ tsp. vanilla	2 mL vanilla

Combine sugar, cornstarch and salt; stir in milk. Cook until thick, stirring constantly. Mix egg and juice. Stir in a little of hot mixture — then pour back into hot mixture. Cook over low heat, stirring for 2 minutes. Add peel, butter and vanilla.

COCONUT CRUST:

1¼ cups shredded coconut	300 mL shredded coconut
¾ cup graham cracker crumbs	175 mL graham cracker crumbs
½ cup sugar	125 mL sugar
½ cup flour	125 mL flour
½ cup soft butter or margarine	125 mL soft butter or margarine

Mix these ingredients. Place half in 9 x 9" (2.5 L) pan. Pour in filling; top with remaining crust mixture. Bake at 375°F-400°F (190°C-200°C) for 25 minutes until top is golden brown. Makes 9 servings.

ALMOND CARROT CAKE

½ cup butter or margarine	125 mL butter or margarine
1 cup sugar	250 mL sugar
3 eggs	3 eggs
½ cup milk	125 mL milk
1½ tbsp. lemon juice	20 mL lemon juice
1½ cups finely grated carrots	375 mL finely grated carrots
1 cup almonds, ground fine	250 ml almonds, ground fine
1½ cups flour	375 mL flour
2½ tsp. baking powder	12 mL baking powder
1 tsp. salt	5 mL salt
1½ tsp. cinnamon	7 mL cinnamon
½ tsp. nutmeg	2 mL nutmeg
½ cup unsweetened coconut	125 mL unsweetened coconut
½ cup chocolate chips	125 mL chocolate chips
tangy sauce . . . recipe follows	tangy sauce . . . recipe follows

Cream butter or margarine with the sugar. Beat in eggs. Add milk, lemon juice, carrots and almonds.

Combine the flour, baking powder, salt and spices. Add to the creamed mixture. Finally, fold in the coconut and chips.

Bake in a greased tube pan or 9 x 13" (3.5 L) baking pan. Bake at 350°F (180°C) for 45 minutes-1 hour, or until a toothpick inserted in the center comes out clean.

Slice and serve with tangy sauce, or cover with icing and have as regular cake.

TANGY SAUCE

½ cup sugar	125 mL sugar
1½ tbsp. cornstarch	20 mL cornstarch
dash of salt	dash of salt
1½ cups boiling water	375 mL boiling water
2 tbsp. butter	25 mL butter
1 lemon, juice and grated rind	1 lemon, juice and grated rind

In a medium saucepan, combine the sugar, cornstarch and salt. Slowly add the boiling water and cook over medium heat until the mixture thickens and is clear. Stir all the while.

Remove from heat and stir in the butter and lemon juice and rind.

Serve hot over slices of the carrot cake, or over anything else that might appreciate a bright fresh sauce!

RHUBARB UPSIDE DOWN CAKE

3 cups sliced rhubarb	750 mL sliced rhubarb
1½ cups miniature marshmallows	375 mL miniature marshmallows
¾ cup sugar	175 mL sugar
½ cup butter or margarine	125 mL butter or margarine
1 cup sugar	250 mL sugar
2 eggs	2 eggs
1¾ cups flour	425 mL flour
3 tsp. baking powder	15 mL baking powder
½ tsp. salt	2 mL salt
¼ cup milk	50 mL milk
1 tsp. vanilla	5 mL vanilla

Grease an 8 x 8" (2 L) cake pan. Spread the prepared rhubarb in the bottom of the pan; then sprinkle with marshmallows and ¾ cup (175 mL) sugar.

Cream butter and 1 cup (250 mL) sugar until fluffy. Add eggs one at a time, beating well after each addition.

Mix flour, baking powder and salt together. Add to creamed mixture alternately with milk and vanilla. Batter will be very thick. Drop batter by small teaspoons on rhubarb mixture and spread as evenly as possible.

Bake about 50 minutes in 350°F (180°C) oven until top of cake springs back when touched lightly in the centre. Let stand in pan 5 minutes, then invert on serving plate. Leave the pan over the cake for a few minutes to allow all the juices to run out.

Serve with whipped cream or ice cream.

BLUEBERRY HAPPY BOYS

2 cups blueberries	500 ml blueberries
¾ cup sugar	175 mL sugar
¾ cup water	175 mL water
2 cups flour	500 ml flour
1 tbsp. sugar	15 mL sugar
¼ tsp. salt	1 mL salt
4 tsp. baking powder	20 mL baking powder
3 tbsp. shortening	50 mL shortening
⅔ cup milk	150 mL milk

Combine blueberries, sugar and water. Bring to a boil and boil 3 minutes.

Meanwhile, mix and sift dry ingredients. Cut in the shortening; add milk to make a soft dough.

Drop by spoonfuls into the stewing blueberries as you would dumplings. Cover and cook for 10 minutes, or until done.

Serve warm. Serves 6 people.

DAWN'S STRAWBERRY CHEESECAKE

1¼ cups crushed graham wafers	300 mL crushed graham wafers
⅓ cup melted butter	75 mL melted butter
¼ cup sugar	50 mL sugar
1 lb. cream cheese, room temp.	500 g cream cheese, room temp.
¾ cup sugar	175 mL sugar
3 eggs	3 eggs
1 tsp. vanilla	5 mL vanilla
1 lb. frozen strawberries*	500 g frozen strawberries*
1 tbsp. lemon juice	15 mL lemon juice
1 tbsp. cornstarch	15 mL cornstarch
few drops red food colouring	few drops red food colouring

Crush the graham wafers, add the melted butter and ¼ cup (50 mL) sugar. Mix lightly and press into a greased 9 x 9" square pan (2.5 L). Pyrex works well for many people. Just spread across the bottom of the pan; don't try to work it up the edges.

Beat together the cream cheese, sugar, eggs and vanilla. Blend thoroughly. Pour over the crust and bake 1 hour at 275ºF (140ºC), or until done. Remove from heat and cool.

In a small saucepan, mix the strawberries, lemon juice and cornstarch. Cook over medium heat until the mixture thickens and becomes transparent. Add red colouring, if desired. Remove from heat, cool and pour over cooled cake.

Serve as is, or freeze as is. It will be like new when thawed for later use.

*Frozen strawberries are generally already sweetened, so you needn't add sugar at this stage. If they're not, add ½ cup sugar.

CHOCOLATE CHEESECAKE

CRUST

1 cup graham wafer crumbs	250 mL graham wafer crumbs
¼ cup cocoa	50 mL cocoa
2 tbsp. sugar	30 mL sugar
¼ cup melted butter	50 mL melted butter

Combine crumbs, cocoa, sugar and melted butter. Press into 7" (18 cm) springform pan over the bottom and halfway up the sides. Chill while making filling.

FILLING:

16 oz. cream cheese	500 g cream cheese
½ cup sugar	125 mL sugar
2 eggs	2 eggs
6 oz. semi-sweet chocolate, melted and cooled	175 g semi-sweet chocolate melted and cooled
1 tsp. almond flavouring	5 mL almond flavouring
1 tsp. vanilla	5 mL vanilla
⅓ cup orange liqueur	75 mL orange liqueur
½ cup sour cream	125 mL sour cream

Beat cream cheese until smooth; beat in sugar. Beat in eggs one at a time at low speed. Add cooled chocolate, flavourings, liqueur and sour cream. Beat at low speed until blended. Pour over crumbs in pan.

Bake at 300°F (150°C) for 1 hour. Turn off heat and leave cake in oven for one more hour. Cool at room temperature and then chill at least 24 hours in refrigerator.

TOPPING:

2 oz. semi-sweet chocolate	1 square of semi-sweet chocolate
1 tsp. butter	5 mL butter
whipped cream	whipped cream
toasted sliced almonds	toasted sliced almonds

Melt chocolate and butter together. Spread over cheesecake. Garnish with whipped cream and almonds.

Cakes

The Ladies' Aid Tea

Counterclockwise from back:
Peggy's Walnut Chiffon Cake
Marble Pound Cake
Mom's Jelly Roll
Vinetarta
Carrot Cake With a Difference

Community dances were a little bit of dancing, a little bit of communing, and a whole lot of fun!

Food, of course, was always part of the general plan.

The ladies brought sandwiches and a sweet of some sort — cookies or cake. Around about 11:30, they would make the coffee, set out the food, dust out the cups and wait for the supper waltz.

By the way, it was the married women who made all these preparations. They had the time since the supper waltz was more or less decided for them — they'd have to dance it with their husbands. What else did you have a husband for, after all?

But the single girls — they couldn't begin to think of anything so mundane as lunch arrangements until their own lunch arrangements had been made . . . that is, until somebody asked them for the supper waltz. It was always sweet agony waiting for those sensitive arrangements to be completed!

A young women could not, in those days, be so bold as to ask a young man to dance with her. She had to do it in much sneakier ways — like smiling a lot and looking at the right young man at just the right moment. Eventually, by some means or other, most everyone would get paired off and lunch would be served.

Thus, for the singles, the food was an anti-climax. Not so for people like Uncle Carl who batched and definitely preferred someone else's cooking to his own. He used to get right up front when the food was passed around at dances, and as long as it was passed, he kept on eating.

Sandwiches were, more often than not, bologna but on homemade bread, that tasted pretty good. Sometimes you'd find a beef or ham or salmon, but they were few and far between.

Cakes were pretty standard in the very early days too. Margie's Mom gave us the recipe for the epitome of hard times cake (page 121). It uses tallow or drippings for shortening, snow in place of eggs and water instead of milk.

It must have been a rather heavy duty number but she laughs when she thinks of those days. Her sturdy cake then was as welcome as all the light fluffy wonders available now. Everything is relative.

The coffee made at a dance or chicken supper was made by dumping one pound of coffee into a boilerful of cold water and then setting the boiler on the air-tight heater until everything came to a full rolling boil. Then the boiler was set onto the back of the heater so that the grounds could settle . . . and that was your basic boiled coffee. Finest kind, people remember today.

A cake was the focus of one of the community's favourite stories. It seems that the Dixonville ladies were asked to provide a nice lunch for the judges at the Beaton Creek exhibition one year . . . although why they'd need a lunch after sampling dozens of pies, cakes, cookies, fudge, etc., I can't imagine.

Anyway, the Dixonville ladies tackled the job with a determination to give them an unforgettable lunch. After all, the five or six ladies of note from Peace River and the district agriculturist did the job for nothing, so it was reasoned that the least they could do was feed them well.

The lunch was arranged on a cloth covered table under some shade trees behind the hall. The crowning glory, a beautifully iced layer cake, was uncovered and put on display. Everything was ready.

Just then the doors of the hall opened to signal the end of judging. Everyone rushed in to see how their entries had fared, leaving the table and its contents unattended for a few minutes.

Sure enough, McGrath's old dog Mike ate the cake.

In our family, Dad was the first cake maker and he still likes to whip up his favourite — the boiled raisin cake. Mrs. Banks taught him how to make it in the early thirties and he has relied on that recipe ever since. It's an eggless, butterless, milkless marvel that turns out remarkably well in spite of its deprivations. The original boiled raisin cake is on page 132 and is called Johnnie's Christmas Cake.

When kids came along and slightly better times, Mom branched out into more complicated cakes. She never could go beyond one cup of shortening and two cups of sugar however. Her depression memories were just too close for comfort. Even now if a recipe calls for two cups of raisins, say, she cuts the amount by at least one-half a cup.

Her kids sometimes go the other extreme so you'll find recipes in the next section that range from the sternly sensible to the slightly extravagant. Only slightly extravagant though . . . we are our mother's daughters. Read, eat and enjoy!

HARD TIMES CAKE

1 cup sugar	250 mL sugar
½ cup tallow or drippings	125 mL tallow or drippings
1 cup milk or water	250 mL milk or water
1 tsp. vanilla, if available	5 mL vanilla, if available
½ tsp. salt	2 mL salt
1½ cups flour	375 mL flour
2 tsp. baking powder	10 mL baking powder
2 heaping tbsp. snow	30 mL snow

Cream the sugar and tallow or drippings. Add the milk if the cow is still functioning; otherwise, add water. If vanilla is available, add it.

Mix together the salt, flour and baking powder. Stir into the creamed mixture. Finally, quickly stir in the snow. It replaces the rising action of eggs since hens seldom lay in the middle of winter.

Bake in a greased pan until done. Frost if you have the makings. Otherwise, make the best of it!

You could also add a handful of raisins or currants, if they are available. Fresh fruits also add flavour in the summer months. This is very much a do-it-yourself cake.

BOILED RAISIN CAKE

2 cups raisins	500 mL raisins
2 cups brown sugar	500 mL brown sugar
2 cups water	500 mL water
2 tsp. cinnamon	10 mL cinnamon
1 tsp. cloves	5 mL cloves
1 tsp. nutmeg	5 mL nutmeg
1 tsp. allspice	5 mL allspice
1 tsp. ginger	5 mL ginger
½ cup lard	125 mL lard
2 tsp. soda	10 mL soda
2 tsp. salt	10 mL salt
2 tsp. baking powder	10 mL baking powder
2 cups flour	500 mL flour
1 cup fruit or nuts	250 mL fruit or nuts
2 eggs	2 eggs

Boil the first nine ingredients together in a large saucepan. Cool completely. This takes awhile.

Mix dry ingredients with fruit or nuts. Beat the eggs and add to cooled mixture. Then add the dry ingredients and stir well.

Bake in 8" (2 L) tube pan which has been well greased and floured. Bake at 350°F (180°C) for 50-60 minutes or until toothpick inserted in centre comes out clean. Let cool for 10 minutes and remove from pan.

MOM'S JELLY ROLL

3 eggs	3 eggs
1 cup white sugar	250 mL white sugar
1 tsp. vanilla or almond flavouring	5 mL vanilla or almond flavouring
1 cup flour	250 mL flour
1 tsp. baking powder	5 mL baking powder
½ cup boiling water	125 mL boiling water

Grease and flour a jelly roll pan — a pan about 9 x 15" (25 x 40 cm) with edges high enough to hold the batter. Line with greased wax paper as well.

Beat eggs well, gradually add the sugar and continue beating until the mixture is light and creamy. Stir in flavouring. Mix together the flour and baking powder and add gradually to the egg mixture, beating well. Stir in boiling water. Pour carefully into prepared pan. Bake in 350ºF (180ºC) oven about 15 minutes or until the cake is browned and springs back when touched.

Have a clean tea towel ready. Dampen it slightly and then spread it on a flat surface. Sprinkle with sugar. Loosen the cake around the edges and let it fall gradually out of the pan onto the tea towel. Once out of the pan, spread it with a tart jelly — or lemon butter — or apple butter — or whatever you have to use up. Roll up. To serve, slice in generous portions.

CHOCOLATE CAKE

1 cup brown sugar	250 mL brown sugar
½ cup cocoa	125 mL cocoa
1 cup buttermilk	250 mL buttermilk
½ cup butter or margarine	125 mL butter or margarine
1 cup white sugar	250 mL white sugar
2 eggs, well beaten	2 eggs, well beaten
1 cup buttermilk	250 mL buttermilk
1 tsp. baking soda	5 mL baking soda
2 cups flour	500 mL flour
½ tsp. salt	2 mL salt
1 tsp. vanilla	5 mL vanilla

Blend the brown sugar, ½ cup (125 mL) cocoa and 1 cup (250 mL) buttermilk in a saucepan and bring to a boil. Stir well to dissolve sugar. Set aside to cool.

Cream butter or margarine with white sugar until light and fluffy. Add well beaten eggs and beat again. Add the cooled chocolate mixture gradually and beat again.

Stir soda into the remaining buttermilk and add to the creamed mixture alternately with the flour. Add salt and vanilla.

Bake in a large baking pan, approximately 9 x 13" (3.5 L) or in a tube pan. Grease and flour before pouring in the batter. Bake in 350ºF (180ºC) oven for 40-50 minutes, or until done. Frost when cool.

FROSTING:

½ cup soft butter	125 mL soft butter
½ cup cocoa	125 mL cocoa
3 cups icing sugar	750 mL icing sugar
4 tbsp. warm milk or cream	50 mL warm milk or cream
1½ tsp. vanilla	7 mL vanilla

Cream butter until fluffy. Stir together cocoa and icing sugar. Add alternately to butter with warm milk or cream and vanilla.

CARROT CAKE WITH A DIFFERENCE

1 cup oil	250 mL oil
2 cups sugar	500 mL sugar
1 tsp. cinnamon	5 mL cinnamon
¼ tsp. nutmeg	1 mL nutmeg
4 eggs	4 eggs
1 tsp. vanilla	5 mL vanilla
2 cups flour	500 mL flour
2 tsp. baking powder	10 mL baking powder
1 tsp. salt	5 mL salt
1½ tsp. baking soda	7 mL baking soda
1 can crushed pineapple, drained (8 oz.)	1 can crushed pineapple, drained (250 g)
2 cups grated raw carrot	500 mL grated raw carrot
1 cup nuts, chopped	250 mL nuts, chopped

Mix together the oil, sugar, cinnamon, nutmeg, eggs and vanilla. Combine flour, baking powder, salt and baking soda. Add to the first mixture. Finally, fold in the pineapple, raw carrot and nuts.

Bake in a large 9 x 13" (3.5 L) pan or two layer cake pans or in an angel food pan. Bake at 350ºF (180ºC) for 35-50 minutes, depending on the depth of the pan. Check after half an hour. You don't want to dry out the cake. That is the point of carrot cake; it is one of the moistest cakes going. When cool, ice with cream cheese icing. Some people think it's the best part of the cake!

ICING:

1 pkg. (8 oz.) cream cheese	1 pkg. (250 g) cream cheese
¼ cup butter or margarine	50 mL butter or margarine
1 lb. icing sugar	500 g icing sugar
1 tsp. vanilla	5 mL vanilla

Soften the cream cheese and work the butter or margarine in until smooth and well blended. Then add the icing sugar and vanilla. Mix until smooth.

SAUERKRAUT CHOCOLATE CAKE

2¼ cups flour	550 mL flour
½ cup cocoa	125 mL cocoa
1 tsp. baking powder	5 mL baking powder
1 tsp. baking soda	5 mL baking soda
¼ tsp. salt	1 mL salt
⅔ cup butter or margarine	150 mL butter or margarine
1½ cups sugar	375 mL sugar
3 eggs	3 eggs
1 tsp. vanilla	5 mL vanilla
1 cup water or strong coffee	250 mL water or strong coffee
⅔ cup sauerkraut, drained and finely chopped	150 mL sauerkraut, drained and finely chopped

Combine the first five ingredients. In a large bowl, cream the butter and add the sugar, mixing well. Then add the eggs one at a time, beating well after each. Add vanilla.

Add the dry ingredients alternately with the water or coffee, beginning and ending with dry ingredients. Rinse, drain and finely chop sauerkraut. Add to the batter and mix thoroughly.

Bake in 2 greased and floured 8" (20 cm) round cake pans or in a larger rectangular pan at 350°F (180°C) for 25-30 minutes, or until done.

SUSAN'S WINNING WHITE CAKE

2 cups flour	500 mL flour
2½ tsp. baking powder	15 mL baking powder
½ tsp. salt	2 mL salt
1 cup sugar	250 mL sugar
3 egg whites	3 egg whites
¼ cup sugar	50 mL sugar
½ cup shortening	125 mL shortening
¾ cup milk	175 mL milk
1 tsp. vanilla	5 mL vanilla

Mix the flour, baking powder, salt and 1 cup (250 mL) sugar. Beat egg whites until foamy; then begin to add the ¼ cup (50 mL) sugar and continue beating until the whites will hold up in peaks.

Place shortening in a bowl and stir to soften. Add dry ingredients alternately with the milk. Stir thoroughly. Add vanilla. Finally, add the egg white mixture and beat well. This is not a folding situation — beat the batter at this stage.

Turn into two greased layer cake pans and bake in 350°F (180°C) oven for 25-30 minutes or until done. Frost as desired. This is a nice white evenly textured cake. It is a good one for a birthday when you want to put a little extra effort into the final product.

MRS. JOHNSON'S RHUBARB CAKE

½ cup butter or margarine
1½ cups brown sugar
1 egg, beaten
2 cups flour
1 tsp. baking soda
¼ tsp. salt
1 cup buttermilk
1 tsp. vanilla
1½-2 cups finely chopped raw
  rhubarb
½ cup white sugar
1 tsp. cinnamon

125 mL butter or margarine
375 mL brown sugar
1 egg, beaten
500 mL flour
5 mL baking soda
1 mL salt
250 mL buttermilk
5 mL vanilla
375-500 mL finely chopped raw
  rhubarb
125 mL white sugar
5 mL cinnamon

Cream shortening and brown sugar; add beaten egg and mix well. Mix the flour, baking soda and salt together and add to the creamed mixture alternately with the buttermilk. Add vanilla.

Fold in the rhubarb. Rhubarb should be in small chunks and should be fresh and tender. If using frozen, let it thaw first and if there is juice formed during the thawing process, make it part of the liquid. In other words, there should be one cup of liquid — whether it is all buttermilk or part buttermilk, part rhubarb juice.

Put into an 8 x 8" (2 L) greased cake pan. Sprinkle with the mixture of white sugar and cinnamon. Bake in 350ºF (180ºC) oven for 40-45 minutes, or until done.

Very good warm, but nice and moist for longer periods of time.

TOMATO SOUP CAKE

1 cup butter or margarine
¾ cup sugar
2 eggs
2 cups flour
4 tsp. baking powder
1 tsp. baking soda
1 tsp. allspice
½ tsp. cinnamon
¼ tsp. cloves
1 can (10 oz.) tomato soup
3 tbsp. water
1 cup raisins
½ cup walnuts, chopped

250 mL butter or margarine
175 mL sugar
2 eggs
500 mL flour
20 mL baking powder
5 mL baking soda
5 mL allspice
2 mL cinnamon
1 mL cloves
1 can (284 mL) tomato soup
50 mL water
250 mL raisins
125 mL walnuts, chopped

In a large bowl, cream butter or margarine with sugar. Add eggs, one at a time and beat well.

Mix together the flour, baking powder, baking soda and spices. Add to the creamed mixture alternately with the tomato soup and water, beginning and ending with a dry portion. The batter will be good and thick. Add raisins and nuts last.

Bake in greased 9 x 13" (3.5 L) pan or two 8" (2 L) round cake pans. Bake in 350ºF (180ºC) oven for approximately 30 minutes. Fill and/or frost as you will.

CRUMB CAKE

1½ cups brown sugar	375 mL brown sugar
1½ cups flour	375 mL flour
2 tsp. cinnamon	10 mL cinnamon
1 tsp. nutmeg	5 mL nutmeg
½ tsp. cloves	2 mL cloves
½ tsp. salt	2 mL salt
½ cup butter or margarine	125 mL butter or margarine
1 tsp. baking powder	5 mL baking powder
½ tsp. baking soda	2 mL baking soda
1 egg, beaten	1 egg, beaten
⅔ cup buttermilk	150 mL buttermilk
1 cup raisins	250 mL raisins

Mix together the brown sugar, flour, cinnamon, nutmeg, cloves, and salt. Cut in the butter until the mixture resembles fine crumbs. Set aside ¾ cup (175 mL) of these crumbs.

To the remaining crumbs, add the baking powder and baking soda; then add the beaten egg, buttermilk and raisins. Pour batter into an 8 x 8" (2 L) greased baking pan and top with the reserved crumbs. Bake in 350°F (180°C) oven for 40 minutes, or until toothpick inserted in centre comes out clean.

GINGERBREAD CUP CAKES

½ cup butter	125 mL butter
⅓ cup brown sugar	75 mL brown sugar
2 eggs, well beaten	2 eggs, well beaten
½ cup molasses	125 mL molasses
½ cup milk	125 mL milk
¼ tsp. baking soda	1 mL baking soda
2 tsps. baking powder	10 mL baking powder
½ tsp. salt	2 mL salt
1 tsp. ginger	5 mL ginger
½ tsp. cloves	2 mL cloves
½ tsp. cinnamon	5 mL cinnamon
1¾ cups flour	425 mL flour
⅓ cup raisins (optional)	75 mL raisins (optional)

Cream butter, blend in sugar. Add eggs and beat well. Combine molasses and milk. Add to the creamed mixture alternately with sifted dry ingredients. Finally, fold in raisins, if desired. Fill buttered muffin tins ⅔ full.

Bake in 375°F (190°C) oven for 20 to 25 minutes or until done. Makes 15-20 medium cupcakes.

PEGGY'S WALNUT CHIFFON CAKE

2 cups flour	500 mL flour
¾ cup white sugar	175 mL white sugar
¾ cup brown sugar	175 mL brown sugar
3 tsp. baking powder	15 mL baking powder
1 tsp. salt	5 mL salt
½ cup vegetable oil	125 mL vegetable oil
6 egg yolks, unbeaten	6 egg yolks, unbeaten
¾ cup cold water	175 mL cold water
1 tsp. maple flavouring	5 mL maple flavouring
1 cup egg whites (7 or 8)	250 mL egg whites (7 or 8)
½ tsp. cream of tartar	2 mL cream of tartar
1 cup walnuts, finely chopped	250 mL walnuts, finely chopped

Sift the dry ingredients together. Make a well and add, in order, the oil, egg yolks, cold water and flavouring. Beat until smooth.

Whip the egg whites and cream of tartar until very stiff. A spatula should leave a clear path if pulled through very dry egg whites. Gradually pour the egg yolk mixture over the whites and fold in very carefully. Do not stir. Also, fold in the walnuts very carefully, with as few strokes as possible. Pour into ungreased 10" (3 L) tube pan.

Bake at 325°F (160°C) for an hour; then at 350°F (180°C) for about 10 minutes. Remove from oven and immediately invert on a bottle or otherwise arrange the pan so that it is inverted and free of the counter surface. Ice with Golden Butter Frosting.

GOLDEN BUTTER FROSTING

½ cup butter	125 mL butter
4 cups sifted icing sugar	1 L sifted icing sugar
½ cup light cream	125 mL light cream
1-1½ tsp. maple flavouring	5 mL-7 mL maple flavouring

Melt the butter in saucepan; keep over low heat until golden brown. Watch that it does not scorch.

Remove from heat; stir in sifted icing sugar. Blend in cream and maple flavouring or vanilla. Place pan in ice water and beat until spreading consistency. Add more cream if needed.

This makes a generous portion.

MATRIMONIAL CAKE

1 ¾ cups rolled oats	425 mL rolled oats
1 cup brown sugar	250 mL brown sugar
1 ½ cups flour	375 mL flour
1 tsp. soda	5 mL soda
¼ tsp. salt	1 mL salt
¾ cup butter or margarine	175 mL butter or margarine
½ lb. dates	250 g dates
½ cup sugar	125 mL sugar
1 cup water	250 mL water
juice of 1 lemon	juice of 1 lemon

Mix together the rolled oats, sugar, flour, soda and salt. Rub the butter or margarine in as you would for pie dough. Press half the crumb mixture into a greased 8 x 8" (2 L) baking pan. Cover with the filling.

To make filling, cook the dates, sugar and water together until the mixture is thick and smooth — about 10 minutes. Add lemon juice and mix well. Spread filling over crumbs. Then press the remaining crumbs over the filling. Bake in a 300ºF (150ºC) oven for about 45 minutes, or until lightly browned.

NOT SO TRADITIONAL RAISIN FILLING

½ cup brown sugar	125 mL brown sugar
2 tbsp. cornstarch	30 mL cornstarch
¾ cup water	175 mL water
1 cup raisins	250 mL raisins
peel and juice of 1 lemon	peel and juice of 1 lemon
⅓ cup walnuts, chopped	75 mL walnuts, chopped

Combine sugar, cornstarch, water and raisins and cook over low heat until thickened. Remove from heat and add lemon juice, peel and walnuts.

ANGEL FOOD CAKE

1 cup sifted cake flour	250 mL sifted cake flour
1 ½ cups sugar	375 mL sugar
¼ tsp. salt	1 mL salt
1 ¼ cups egg whites	300 mL egg whites
(about 8 large eggs)	(about 8 large eggs)
1 ⅓ tsp. cream of tartar	8 mL cream of tartar
1 tsp. vanilla	5 mL vanilla
½ tsp. almond extract	2 mL almond extract

Sift flour once, then measure. Add 1 cup (250 mL) sugar and salt.

Beat egg whites until foamy; then add cream of tartar and continue beating until egg whites are stiff enough to stand up firmly. Fold in the other ½ cup (125 mL) sugar gradually. Add flavourings.

Now fold in sugar and flour mixture 3 tbsp. (50 mL) at a time. Pour into ungreased angel food cake tin. Cut batter with a knife to prevent large bubbles.

Bake in 300ºF (150ºC) oven for 15 minutes. Then increase heat to 325ºF (160ºC) and bake for another 1 to 1¼ hours, until the crust appears quite firm to the touch. For best results, do not open oven to check cake for at least first 40 minutes.

POPPY SEED POUNDCAKE

⅓ cup poppy seed	75 mL poppy seed
⅔ cup butter or margarine	150 mL butter or margarine
1¼ cups sugar	300 mL sugar
1 tbsp. grated lemon rind	15 mL grated lemon rind
1 tbsp. lemon juice	15 mL lemon juice
2 cups flour	500 mL flour
1 tsp. salt	5 mL salt
1 tsp. baking powder	5 mL baking powder
⅔ cup milk	150 mL milk
3 eggs	3 eggs
1 tsp. vanilla	5 mL vanilla

Toast the poppy seeds by placing in a pie plate and baking for about 15 minutes in a 350°F (180°C) oven. Shake the plate at five minute intervals throughout the baking process. Set aside to cool.

Cream the shortening with the sugar until light and fluffy. Add lemon rind and lemon juice.

Mix together the flour, salt, baking powder and add alternately to the creamed mixture with the milk. Add eggs, one at a time, beating thoroughly after each.

Pound cakes need to be pounded; in other words, they need to be mixed very thoroughly. Just before pouring into greased loaf pan, add the vanilla and poppy seeds.

Bake in a 300°F (150°C) oven for about 1¼ hours. A crack will likely appear across the top of the poundcake when it is close to done. Test with a toothpick or cake tester.

Cool cake in pan for about 20 minutes; then remove and cool completely on rack. Frost with lemon icing.

LEMON ICING

⅓ cup butter or margarine	75 mL butter or margarine
1 cup icing sugar	250 mL icing sugar
1½ tbsp. milk or cream	20 mL milk or cream
1½ tbsp. lemon juice	20 mL lemon juice
2 cups icing sugar	500 mL icing sugar
grated rind of 1 lemon	grated rind of 1 lemon
1 tbsp. poppy seed	15 mL poppy seed

In a medium bowl with the electric mixer, cream butter or margarine until soft. Gradually beat in 1 cup (250 mL) icing sugar. Then add milk and lemon juice. Gradually beat in the remaining icing sugar, until the frosting is light and fluffy.

Spread on the top and sides of cooled pound cake. Sprinkle lemon rind down the centre of the cake and top that stripe with the additional poppy seeds.

MARBLE POUND CAKE

1 cup butter or margarine	250 mL butter or margarine
2 cups sugar	500 mL sugar
4 eggs	4 eggs
2 tsp. vanilla	10 mL vanilla
3½ cups flour	875 mL flour
1½ tsp. baking powder	7 mL baking powder
dash of salt	dash of salt
1 cup milk	250 mL milk
¼ cup cocoa or	50 mL cocoa or
1 sq. unsweetened chocolate	1 sq. unsweetened chocolate

Soften the butter or margarine and then gradually add the sugar, beating well the whole time. It is important to get the mixture very light and fluffy at this stage. Add eggs one at a time and continue the heavy duty beating. Add vanilla.

Mix together the flour, baking powder, and salt. Add to the creamed mixture alternately with the milk. Again, beat well.

Remove about 2 cups (500 mL) of the batter and put into a smaller bowl. Add the cocoa or melted chocolate and blend well. Grease a tube pan and spoon in about ⅔ of the white cake batter. Blob the chocolate mixture at various places — not all over — and then add the remaining white mixture. Take a spatula and twist through the batters to give a marblized effect. Do not mix thoroughly — just zigzag the spatula through the batter so that both colours are still distinct but marbled together.

Bake in 350°F (180°C) oven for an hour or until toothpick inserted in the centre of the cake comes out clean. Cool and remove from pan. May be iced — doesn't really need it since it is moist and flavourful on its own.

Homemakers were ingenious in the early days — there's no getting around that fact!

If they couldn't get eggs, they used snow or other leavening agents.

If they couldn't get butter, they used lard or drippings.

If they couldn't get sugar, they used molasses or honey, and if they couldn't get them, they did without. (Some people in fact tried to grow sugar beets on their farms to ensure a supply of sugar. The beets grew all right but nobody could figure out how to separate the sugar from the pulp. Generally the cows and pigs benefitted from the sugar beet experiments.)

The following recipe doesn't require shortening so it was used when the cow was dry or the price too high! It's a good basic fruit loaf, good for lunches and light snacks.

BARMBRACK

1 cup hot strong tea	250 mL hot strong tea
½ cup chopped dates	125 mL chopped dates
½ cup chopped mixed peel	125 mL chopped mixed peel
1 cup raisins, washed	250 mL raisins, washed
1 cup brown sugar	250 mL brown sugar
2 cups flour	500 mL flour
1 tsp. baking powder	5 mL baking powder
¼ tsp. soda	1 mL soda
¼ tsp. salt	1 mL salt
1 egg, beaten	1 egg, beaten

Pour the tea over the fruit and sugar and let stand overnight. In the morning, mix together the dry ingredients. Then beat the egg and add it to the fruit and tea mixture. Add the dry ingredients and stir. Pour into greased loaf pan and bake in 300ºF (150ºC) oven for 1½ hours, or until done. Serve sliced, with lots of butter, or serve as is for a nutritious, low calorie snack.

LEMON LOAF

½ cup butter or margarine	125 mL butter or margarine
1 cup white sugar	250 mL white sugar
2 eggs, beaten	2 eggs, beaten
1½ cups flour	375 mL flour
1 tsp. baking powder	5 mL baking powder
½ tsp. salt	2 mL salt
½ cup milk	125 mL milk
grated rind of 1 lemon	grated rind of 1 lemon

TOPPING:

juice of 1 lemon	juice of 1 lemon
¼ cup sugar	50 mL sugar

Cream together the butter or margarine and the sugar. Add the eggs and beat thoroughly. Mix together the flour, baking powder and salt and add to the creamed mixture alternately with the milk. Lastly, add the grated lemon rind.

Pour into greased loaf pan and bake in 350ºF (180ºC) oven for approximately 1 hour.

In the meantime, heat the lemon juice and sugar together until the sugar is completely dissolved. When the loaf comes out of the oven, pour the topping over it. Prick with a toothpick to make sure the lemon topping gets into the cake.

JOHNNIE'S CHRISTMAS CAKE

2 cups brown sugar	500 mL brown sugar
1 cup lard	250 mL lard
2 cups cold water	500 mL cold water
½ tsp. salt	2 mL salt
1 tsp. nutmeg	5 mL nutmeg
1 tsp. cinnamon	5 mL cinnamon
1 tsp. mace	5 mL mace
2 cups raisins	500 mL raisins
1-2 cups other fruit*	250-500 mL other fruit*
4 cups flour	1 L flour
1 tsp. baking powder	5 mL baking powder
2 tsp. soda	10 mL soda

Boil first 9 ingredients for 3 minutes. Cool.

Sift the flour, baking powder and soda into a large bowl. Stir in cooled fruit mixture. Mix well.

Pour into large greased tube pan (2 L or larger). Bake at 350°F (180°C) for about one hour, or until done.

*Fruit suggestions: candied peel, cherries, dates.

DARK CHRISTMAS CAKE

2 lbs. mixed candied fruit	1 kg mixed candied fruit
2 cups seedless raisins	500 mL seedless raisins
2 cups golden raisins	500 mL golden raisins
½ cup brandy or orange juice	125 mL brandy or orange juice
1 cup blanched almonds	250 mL blanched almonds
½ cup flour	125 mL flour
½ cup butter	125 mL butter
¾ cup sugar	175 mL sugar
1 cup packed brown sugar	250 mL packed brown sugar
5 eggs	5 eggs
2 tsp. vanilla	10 mL vanilla
1 tsp. almond flavouring	5 mL almond flavouring
1½ cups flour	375 mL flour
½ tsp. baking soda	2 mL baking soda
½ tsp. each cinnamon & allspice	2 mL each cinnamon & allspice
½ cup strawberry jam	125 mL strawberry jam

Combine candied fruit and raisins. Add brandy or juice and let stand overnight, stirring once or twice.

Prepare cake pan (a round bundt pan or 2 loaf pans). Grease the pan, line with brown paper and grease the paper.

Add almonds to the fruit and toss with ½ cup (125 mL) flour.

Cream butter and white sugar. Add brown sugar and cream thoroughly. Beat in eggs one at a time; add flavourings. Combine remaining flour, soda and spices and blend in. Add strawberry jam and mix well. Mix in floured fruit thoroughly. Turn into prepared pan.

Bake in 275°F (140°C) oven for about 3½ hours or until cake is firm to touch and toothpick inserted in centre comes out clean.

When cooled completely, wrap in foil and store at least two weeks before slicing. If desired, drizzle with brandy or liqueur occasionally to make a really moist cake.

PINEAPPLE FRUITCAKE

1 lb. fruit mix
   (peel, cherries, etc.)
	500 g fruit mix
	   (peel, cherries, etc.)

1 cup crushed pineapple
   with juice
	250 mL crushed pineapple
	   with juice

2 cups light raisins	500 mL light raisins
2 cups slivered almonds	500 mL slivered almonds

1 cup vodka or orange liqueur
   or juice
	250 mL vodka or orange liqueur
	   or juice

1 cup butter or margarine	250 mL butter or margarine
1 cup sugar	250 mL sugar
4 eggs	4 eggs
juice and rind of 1 lemon	juice and rind of 1 lemon
4 cups flour	1 L flour
1 tsp. baking powder	5 mL baking powder
1 tsp. salt	5 mL salt

Soak the fruit mix, pineapple with juice, raisins and almonds in the vodka or liqueur or juice overnight.

Cream the butter or margarine with the sugar. Add the eggs one at a time and beat well after each addition. Add the lemon juice and rind. Combine the flour, baking powder and salt. Add gradually to the creamed mixture, beating well. Fold in the fruit mixture, liquid and all. If the dough looks curdly, add flour by tablespoons until the curdled look disappears.

Grease and flour 3 medium loaf pans. Pour the batter in and bake at 275°F (140°C) for 2½ hours or until done.

GUMDROP CAKE

2 cups gumdrops	500 mL gumdrops
2 cups raisins	500 mL raisins
1 tbsp. flour	15 mL flour
½ cup butter	125 mL butter
1 cup sugar	250 mL sugar
2 eggs, beaten	2 eggs, beaten
2 cups flour	500 mL flour
½ tsp. salt	2 mL salt
1½ tsp. baking powder	7 mL baking powder
1 tsp. cinnamon	5 mL cinnamon
1 tsp. nutmeg	5 mL nutmeg
1 cup milk	250 mL milk

Cut the gumdrops with scissors that have been dipped in cold water. Add the raisins to the gumdrops and flour them with the 1 tbsp. (15 mL) flour.

Cream the butter and sugar; add well beaten eggs. Sift the flour, salt, baking powder, cinnamon and nutmeg and add to the creamed mixture alternately with the milk. Add raisins and gumdrops and mix in.

Bake in greased round cake pans in 350°F (180°C) oven for about 30-40 minutes; in loaf pan for about 1¼ hours. Test before time is up.

Vinetarta

1 cup soft butter	250 mL soft butter
1½ cups sugar	375 mL sugar
2 eggs	2 eggs
4 cups flour	1 L flour
1 tsp. baking powder	5 mL baking powder
3 tbsp. cream	50 mL cream
1 tbsp. almond extract	15 mL almond extract

FILLING:

1½ lbs. prunes	750 g prunes
¾ cup sugar	175 mL sugar
1 tbsp. vanilla	15 mL vanilla
½ cup prune juice	125 mL prune juice
1 tbsp. cinnamon	15 mL cinnamon

Cream the butter and sugar and add the eggs one at a time. Mix the flour and baking powder together and gradually add half to the creamed mixture. Mix in the cream and the flavouring and then add the rest of the flour mixture. Work well with your hands.

Divide the dough into six parts. It is easiest to have six cake pans the same size (canvass your neighbourhood) but if you haven't that many pans or that many neighbours, do it in stages. Pat the six pieces of dough into six round, wax paper lined cake pans. Use your fingers and try to get the dough evenly distributed in the pans. Bake until light brown — about 10-15 minutes at 350ºF (180ºC). Watch carefully. Remove at once from the pans and set on table or counter to cool.

For the filling, cover prunes with water and cook until tender; let cool. Drain off the juice and reserve ½ cup (125 mL) for the filling. Remove the pits and mash the cooked prunes, either with a potato masher or with a blender. (You can start with pitted prunes to make this easier). Put prunes into a saucepan and add the sugar, cinnamon and ½ cup (125 mL) juice. Simmer until thickened. Remove from heat and add vanilla. Cool and spread between layers to produce a 6 layer cake with 5 layers of filling.

The cake is just the right combination of pastry and fruit without adding any icing.

Let ripen for at least three days before using — a week is better. Keep in a tightly sealed container.

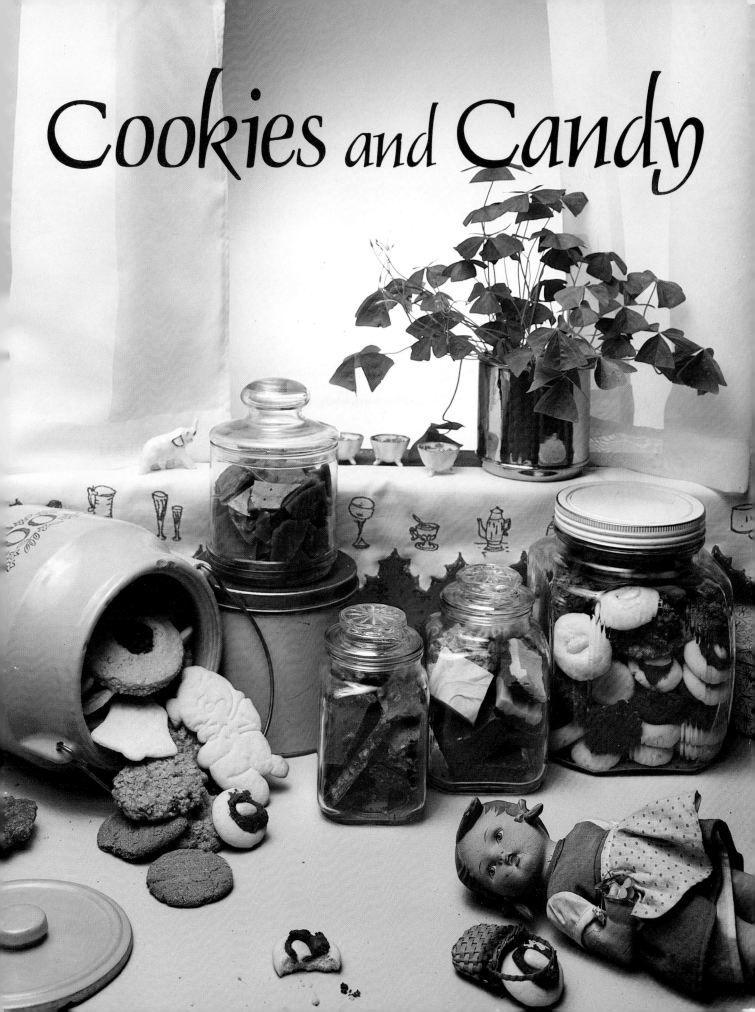

Cookies and Candy

Raiders of the Cookie Jar

Mrs. Laing's Sugar Cookies
Pinwheels
Ginger Cookies
Oatmeal and Raisin Cookies
Chocolate on Chocolate Cookies
Ada's Chocolate Unbaked Cookies
Date Filled Cookies
Brown Eyed Susans
Chinese Almond Cookies
Chocolate Fudge
Fantasy Fudge
Toffee

When Mom had a Ladies' Aid meeting, it was a case of some good news and some bad news.

The bad news was we'd have to clean the house for a week beforehand and put away all our favourite piles of junk.

The good news was that Mom would make poinsettia cookies.

Normally, she went in for no-nonsense big drop cookies. Occasionally, she'd add raisins or dates but generally she stuck with the basic sugar cookie.

But Ladies' Aid deserved better, apparently, and she brought out the cookie press to make at least five different kinds of fancy little cookies. It was great fun for the observers. The fancy cookies didn't taste a whole lot different from the everyday ones but they certainly had more style.

Thus proving the old adage again that it's not what you do but how you do it!

Every fall, each one of us started out with a clean shiny lunch bucket, complete with a functional thermos in the lid. By the end of June, it would be dented, discoloured and more often than not, just plain old disappeared . . . lost forever! For sure, the thermos would be broken. It was a rare bird who could keep a lunch bucket for more than one season!

Lunch time at school was what would now be called "creative play". The teachers generally disappeared, leaving us to our own devices . . . and that's when lunch buckets got thrown out the window or sandwiches stuffed into boots and the like. At one point in elementary school, my classmates and I regularly traded portions of our lunches . . . my sandwich for Helen's, her cookies for Beryl's and so on.

The provincial government decided at one point that these poor little deprived kids on the frontier needed vitamin pills. So they sent us boxes of the things — brown gooey capsules that squirted green stuff if you happened to break the outer shell.

They were probably good for what ailed us but I couldn't swallow the things. I tried everything and ended up sticking them in my sandwiches so that they'd go down with the bread.

Needless to say, this practice ruined sandwiches for me.

It also put a crimp in the exchange programs. Nobody wanted to take the risk of getting a vitamin pill along with their jam sandwich!

Lunches were also necessary for the men in the fields during haying and harvesting — a chore that was one of the most pleasant of all the household chores. For one thing, newly cut hay or grain has a smell like all outdoors — fresh and warm and earthy. Also, the men were generally in a good mood because they were actually bringing in the sheaves, as it were. So they appreciated whatever and whoever arrived.

Lunch usually consisted of sandwiches or buns, cookies or cake and a drink. The cookies were again of the sensible persuasion.

The following section thus begins with the original sensibles but then moves on to brave new cookie worlds as well. We've also included some old and new favourites from the candy world.

Read, eat and enjoy!

MRS. LAING'S SUGAR COOKIES

1 cup butter	250 mL butter
2 cups sugar	500 mL sugar
4 egg yolks	4 egg yolks
¼ cup milk (sweet or sour)	50 mL milk (sweet or sour)
flavouring to taste*	flavouring to taste*
3½ cups flour	875 mL flour
2 tsp. baking powder	10 mL baking powder
¼ tsp. soda	1 mL soda
½ tsp. salt	2 mL salt

Cream butter and sugar. Add egg yolks, milk and flavouring and beat well. To this mixture, add the dry ingredients and mix well.

Roll out dough to ¼" (5 mm) thickness and cut into favourite shapes. Place on cookie sheet and bake at 350ºF (180ºC) for 8-10 minutes or until edges begin to brown.

*A variety of flavourings works well — vanilla, almond, peppermint or nutmeg. Add the flavouring with the milk.

POINSETTIA COOKIES

¾ cup butter or margarine	175 mL butter or margarine
½ cup sugar	125 mL sugar
1 egg, beaten	1 egg, beaten
2 cups flour	500 mL flour
1 tsp. baking powder	5 mL baking powder
pinch of salt	pinch of salt
1 tsp. vanilla	5 mL vanilla

Cream butter until soft and smooth. Add sugar gradually, beating well after each addition. Add beaten egg. Mix the flour, baking powder and salt together and gradually blend into the creamed mixture. Add vanilla.

Roll to about ¼" (5 mm) thickness on a floured board. Cut with a 2" (5 cm) circular cookie cutter. Make four cuts almost to the centre of the cookie at equal distance around the circle. Fold the four points to the centre like a pinwheel. Finish with a piece of candied marashino cherry in the centre.

Bake in 350ºF (180ºC) oven until cookies are just delicately brown — about 10-12 minutes.

The dough is just the right consistency for a cookie press as well. Choose various designs and bake as above.

PINWHEELS

½ cup butter or margarine	125 mL butter or margarine
½ cup sugar	125 mL sugar
1 egg, beaten	1 egg, beaten
1½ cups flour	375 mL flour
½ tsp. baking powder	2 mL baking powder
dash of salt	dash of salt
3 tbsp. milk	50 mL milk
1 square (1 oz.) unsweetened chocolate, melted	1 square (28g) unsweetened chocolate, melted

Cream the shortening and add the sugar gradually. Add the beaten egg and stir well. Mix together the flour, baking powder and salt and add alternately to the creamed mixture with the milk.

Divide the dough into two equal pieces. To one, add the melted chocolate. Mix well. You may have to get your hands into this one.

Roll out the white mixture into a rectangle, about 6 x 12" (15 x 31 cm). Then roll out the chocolate dough the same size as the white dough and place on top of the white dough. Roll the two together like a jelly roll. Chill until cool enough to slice.

Slice in ¼" (5 mm) slices and bake on a greased baking sheet in 350°F (180°C) oven for about 10 minutes, just until the cookies are very delicately brown.

To vary the pinwheel, substitute several dashes of red food coloring instead of the chocolate and produce pink and white pinwheels.

REAL GINGERSNAPS

1 cup sugar	250 mL sugar
½ cup vegetable oil	125 mL vegetable oil
1 egg	1 egg
½ cup molasses	125 mL molasses
2 cups flour	500 mL flour
1 tsp. ginger	5 mL ginger
1 tsp. cinnamon	5 mL cinnamon
1 tsp. baking soda	5 mL baking soda
½ tsp. salt	2 mL salt

Mix the sugar, oil, egg and molasses well. Combine the flour, spices, baking soda and salt. Add to the first mixture.

Chill until firm. Roll into small balls and place on greased cookie sheet. Do not flatten. Bake at 375°F (190°C) for 8-10 minutes or until done. These will flatten and crack just like gingersnaps are supposed to. They will also test your teeth but that's the idea.

GINGER COOKIES

¾ cup vegetable oil	175 mL vegetable oil
1 cup sugar	250 mL sugar
¼ cup molasses	50 mL molasses
1 egg, beaten	1 egg, beaten
2 cups flour	500 mL flour
2 tsp. soda	10 mL soda
¼ tsp. salt	1 mL salt
1 tsp. cinnamon	5 mL cinnamon
1 tsp. cloves	5 mL cloves
1 tsp. ginger	5 mL ginger

Cream shortening and sugar; add molasses and egg. Mix dry ingredients together and add. Mix well.

Form into walnut sized balls and roll in sugar. Bake on greased cookie sheet in 350°F (180°C) oven for about 15 minutes or until done. You can add raisins to these for an interesting change.

JUMBO RAISIN COOKIES

2 cups raisins	500 mL raisins
1 cup water	250 mL water
1 cup shortening	250 mL shortening
2 cups sugar	500 mL sugar
3 eggs	3 eggs
1 tsp. vanilla	5 mL vanilla
4 cups flour	1 L flour
1 tsp. baking powder	5 mL baking powder
1 tsp. baking soda	5 mL baking soda
1 tsp. salt	5 mL salt
1½ tsp. cinnamon	7 mL cinnamon
¼ tsp. nutmeg	1 mL nutmeg
¼ tsp. allspice	1 mL allspice
1 cup chopped nuts (optional)	250 mL chopped nuts (optional)

Boil raisins in water for 5 minutes. Set aside to cool.

Cream next 4 ingredients. Add cooled raisins (juice and all).

Sift dry ingredients. Add to raisin mixture. Add chopped nuts, if desired. Mix well and drop by teaspoonfuls on a greased baking sheet. Bake at 375°F (190°C) for 12-15 minutes or until done. Makes about 4 dozen. Good lunch box treat.

SOFT MOLASSES COOKIES

2¼ cups flour	550 mL flour
2 tsp. baking powder	10 mL baking powder
1½ tsp. cinnamon	7 mL cinnamon
½ tsp. ginger	2 mL ginger
¼ tsp. salt	1 mL salt
¾ cup raisins	175 mL raisins
⅔ cup margarine	150 mL margarine
½ cup brown sugar	125 mL brown sugar
½ cup molasses	125 mL molasses
1 egg	1 egg
⅓ cup milk	75 mL milk
1½ tsp. vinegar	7 mL vinegar

Combine the flour, baking powder, spices, salt and raisins.

Cream the margarine; add the brown sugar and molasses. Add the egg. Mix the milk and vinegar together and add alternately to the creamed mixture with the dry ingredients. Drop spoonfuls on a greased cookie sheet and bake at 350°F (180°C) for 12-15 minutes or until done.

OATMEAL AND RAISIN COOKIES

1½ cups margarine	375 mL margarine
2 cups brown sugar, packed	500 mL brown sugar, packed
1 cup white sugar	250 mL white sugar
2 eggs	2 eggs
½ cup water	125 mL water
2 tsp. vanilla	10 mL vanilla
2 cups flour	500 mL flour
2 tsp. salt	10 mL salt
2 tsp. cinnamon	10 mL cinnamon
1 tsp. soda	5 mL soda
½ tsp. cloves	2 mL cloves
2 cups raisins	500 mL raisins
1 cup chopped nuts	250 mL chopped nuts
6 cups quick oats	1.5 L quick oats

Mix margarine, sugars, eggs, water and vanilla. Stir in remaining ingredients. Drop dough by rounded teaspoonfuls onto greased cookie sheet.

Bake in 350°F (180°C) oven for 12-15 minutes or until slightly browned. Immediately remove from cookie sheet.

Store in tight container or freeze extra. Makes about 8 dozen.

OATMEAL/COCONUT CRISPS

2 cups butter or margarine	500 mL butter or margarine
2 cups brown sugar	500 mL brown sugar
1 cup white sugar	250 mL white sugar
2 tsp. vanilla	10 mL vanilla
4 eggs	4 eggs
3 cups flour	750 mL flour
2 tsp. salt	10 mL salt
2 tsp. baking soda	10 mL baking soda
6 cups quick oats	1.5 L quick oats
1½ cups flaked coconut	375 mL flaked coconut

Cream butter or margarine and sugars; add eggs and vanilla. Beat well. Add dry ingredients and mix well. Drop by teaspoonfuls onto greased cookie sheet and bake at 350°F (180°C) for 10-15 minutes or until done.

This cookie dough may be kept in a tightly sealed container in the refrigerator for several days to bake fresh as needed. The coconut may be omitted and replaced by raisins or chocolate chips.

CHRISTMAS FRUIT DROPS

½ cup butter or margarine	125 mL butter or margarine
1 cup brown sugar	250 mL brown sugar
2 eggs	2 eggs
2 cups flour	500 mL flour
2 tsp. baking powder	10 mL baking powder
¼ tsp. baking soda	1 mL baking soda
¼ tsp. salt	1 mL salt
½ cup milk	125 mL milk
½ tsp. almond extract	2 mL almond extract
½ cup light raisins	125 mL light raisins
½ cup chopped maraschino cherries	125 mL chopped maraschino cherries
¼ cup mixed peel	50 mL mixed peel
¼ cup candied ginger	50 mL candied ginger
¼ cup chopped almonds	50 mL chopped almonds
2 tbsp. flour	30 mL flour

Cream the butter or margarine and sugar. Add the eggs one at a time and beat well after each addition.

Mix together the flour, baking powder, baking soda and salt and add to the creamed mixture alternately with the milk. Add the almond extract. Put the fruits and nuts into a bowl and sprinkle 2 tbsp. (30 mL) flour over them, just enough to keep them from sticking together. Add to the creamed mixture.

Drop by spoonfuls on a greased baking sheet. Leave some space between the cookies because they tend to flatten out. Bake in 350°F (180°C) oven for 12-15 minutes or until done.

CHERRY FLIPS

½ cup butter or margarine	125 mL butter or margarine
¼ cup icing sugar	50 mL icing sugar
1 egg yolk	1 egg yolk
1 tsp. almond flavouring	5 mL almond flavouring
1 cup flour	250 mL flour
pinch of salt	pinch of salt
maraschino cherries, drained	maraschino cherries, drained

Mix the butter or margarine with the icing sugar. Add the egg yolk and flavouring. Blend in the flour and salt. Drain the cherries very well — blot out on towelling, if necessary.

Wrap a piece of dough around a cherry — just enough to cover it. These cookies are generally included in plates of special goodies so make them as dainty as possible. Place on an ungreased cookie sheet and bake in 350°F (180°C) oven for 15 minutes or until done.

To make these even more special, ice them with a dab of butter icing made with some of the juice from the cherries.

CHOCOLATE ON CHOCOLATE COOKIES

⅔ cup butter or margarine	150 mL butter or margarine
1 cup sugar	250 mL sugar
1 egg	1 egg
1 tsp. vanilla	5 mL vanilla
½ cup cocoa	125 mL cocoa
½ cup buttermilk (or water)	125 mL buttermilk (or water)
1¾ cups flour	425 mL flour
½ tsp. baking soda	2 mL baking soda
½ tsp. salt	2 mL salt
1 cup semi-sweet chocolate chips	250 mL semi-sweet chocolate chips

Cream the butter or margarine with the sugar. Add the egg and vanilla. Beat well.

In a small bowl, mix the cocoa and buttermilk (or water) until the mixture is smooth and all lumps of cocoa have been worked out. Add to the creamed mixture. Combine the dry ingredients and add to the creamed mixture. Finally, add the chocolate chips.

Drop by teaspoonfuls on an ungreased cookie sheet and bake for 8-10 minutes at 350°F (180°C) or until done. You don't want the cookies to get too dry — remove while the centres are still a bit soft. Remove from pan immediately.

These are rich cookies, good enough for special occasions. If there is not time for a chocolate cake, make these and serve warm.

ADA'S CHOCOLATE UNBAKED COOKIES

2 cups white sugar	500 mL white sugar
½ cup butter	125 mL butter
½ cup milk	125 mL milk
1 tsp. vanilla	5 mL vanilla
½ tsp. salt	2 mL salt
3 cups rolled oats	750 mL rolled oats
½ cup cocoa	125 mL cocoa
1 cup coconut	250 mL coconut

Bring first three ingredients to a rolling boil in a heavy pot. Remove from heat. Stir in remaining ingredients and drop by spoonfuls on wax paper to cool.

DATE FILLED COOKIES

1 cup butter or margarine	250 mL butter or margarine
1 cup brown sugar	250 mL brown sugar
½ cup milk	125 mL milk
2 cups oatmeal	500 mL oatmeal
1¾ cups flour	425 mL flour
1 tbsp. baking powder	15 mL baking powder
½ tsp. salt	2 mL salt

FILLING:

3 cups pitted dates	750 mL pitted dates
⅔ cup water	150 ml water
¼ cup sugar	50 mL sugar
1 tsp. lemon juice	5 mL lemon juice

Cream shortening with sugar until light and fluffy. Add milk and mix well. Stir in the oatmeal. Mix together the flour, baking powder and salt. Add slowly to the creamed mixture. Dough will be soft. Chill thoroughly.

Combine the dates, water and sugar. Cook until thick, stirring well. Add the lemon juice. Let cool.

On a floured board, roll out dough about ¼" (5 mm) thick and cut with cookie cutter.

On well greased cookie sheet, arrange cookie bottoms. Place spoonfuls of filling on each. Then cut a thimble hole in each top piece and arrange over the filling. Seal the edges with a fork. Bake about 10 minutes in 350°F (180°C) oven, or until nicely browned.

PEANUT BUTTER COOKIES

1 cup peanut butter	250 mL peanut butter
1 cup white sugar	250 mL white sugar
1 tsp. vanilla	5 mL vanilla
1 egg, beaten	1 egg, beaten

Mix all four ingredients together until well blended. Drop by teaspoonfuls onto an ungreased cookie sheet.

Bake at 350ºF (160ºC) for about 12 minutes. Don't overbake.

Very quick and very peanut buttery!

NANA'S SHORTBREAD

2 cups butter	500 mL butter
1 cup icing sugar	250 mL icing sugar
1 cup cornstarch	250 mL cornstarch
3 cups flour	750 mL flour

Cream the butter and sugar very well, making sure it is light and the sugar completely dissolved. Sift the cornstarch and flour together and add slowly to the creamed mixture, blending well each time. Use hands, if necessary. If the dough is too light, add up to ½ cup (125 mL) additional flour. Toss lightly on a floured board; roll and cut into various shapes. This shortbread is best if rolled fairly thick.

Bake in 350ºF (180ºC) oven for 10 minutes, or until lightly browned.

Shortbread was — and is — a favourite . . . particularly at Christmastime but in some households all year round as well. Karen's mother-in-law regularly keeps some on hand.

In assembling the recipes for this book, it was interesting to discover that most of the shortbread recipes were exactly the same. We got this recipe from at least five different sources . . . which seems to prove that housewives had their way of getting information even in the early days! A good recipe knew no limits or boundaries.

As long as the old milk cow held up, butter was readily available for farm housewives. Town and city housewives had to be more sparing in their use of butter . . . but both town and country knew a good recipe when they tasted one!

THIMBLE COOKIES

Also known as birdsnests, thumbprint cookies and jelly dimples. Also known as fiddly, but worth it.

½ cup margarine or butter	125 mL margarine or butter
¼ cup sugar	50 mL sugar
1 egg yolk, well beaten	1 egg yolk, well beaten
2 tsp. lemon juice	10 mL lemon juice
1 cup flour	250 mL flour
1 egg white, slightly beaten	1 egg white, slightly beaten
1 cup chopped walnuts	250 mL chopped walnuts

Cream the butter or margarine with the sugar and add the egg yolk and lemon juice. Beat well. Add the flour bit by bit and keep mixing thoroughly.

Shape the dough into small balls — about 1" (2.5 cm) in diameter. Dip the balls into the slightly beaten egg white and from there into the chopped walnuts. Place on a greased baking sheet. Make a fairly deep indentation in each ball — with a thimble or slim finger. Then bake at 350ºF (180ºC) for 10-15 minutes or until nicely browned.

If you have the time and the inclination, take the cookies out halfway through the baking process and reinforce the depressions.

If you haven't either of the above, indent the holes immediately when you take the cookies out of the oven. Let them cool and fill with a brightly colored jelly or jam.

CHINESE ALMOND COOKIES

1 cup lard or shortening	250 mL lard or shortening
½ cup white sugar	125 mL white sugar
¼ cup firmly packed brown sugar	50 mL firmly packed brown sugar
1 egg	1 egg
1 tsp. almond extract	5 mL almond extract
2¼ cups flour	550 mL flour
dash of salt	dash of salt
1½ tsp. baking powder	7 mL baking powder
whole blanched almonds	whole blanched almonds
1 egg yolk	1 egg yolk
2 tbsp. water	25 mL water

Cream lard or shortening with sugars until fluffy. Add egg and flavouring.

Mix flour, salt and baking powder together and add to creamed mixture. Blend well.

Roll cookies into size of walnut. Place on ungreased cookie sheet and flatten with a glass. Then press an almond into the centre of each round and brush tops with the mixture of egg yolk and water.

Bake in 350ºF (180ºC) oven for 10-12 minutes or until done.

BROWN EYED SUSANS

¾ cup butter or margarine	175 mL butter or margarine
½ cup sugar	125 mL sugar
1 egg	1 egg
1 tsp. vanilla	5 mL vanilla
1¾ cup flour	425 mL flour
dash of salt	dash of salt

Cream butter or margarine with sugar. Add egg and vanilla and beat until everything is light and fluffy. Add flour and salt and blend well.

Shape dough into small balls (if too soft to handle, chill for 20 minutes or so). Place on ungreased cookie sheet. Make a slight indentation with thumb or thimble. Bake at 350°F (180°C) for 8-10 minutes or until firm and lightly browned. Fill with spoonful of chocolate filling; top with an almond.

CHOCOLATE FILLING:

1 cup icing sugar	250 mL icing sugar
3 tbsp. cocoa	50 mL cocoa
2 tbsp. butter	25 mL butter
½ tsp. vanilla	2 mL vanilla
1½ tbsp. milk	20 mL milk

Combine all ingredients and blend until smooth and creamy.

SUGAR BALLS

1 can (14 oz.) sweetened condensed milk	1 can (395 g) sweetened condensed milk
1 pkg. (6 oz.) strawberry jelly powder	1 pkg. (170 g) strawberry jelly powder
1½ cups unsweetened fine coconut	375 mL unsweetened fine coconut
1 cup vanilla wafer crumbs	250 mL vanilla wafer crumbs
1 pkg. (3 oz.) strawberry jelly powder	1 pkg. (85 g) strawberry jelly powder
whole cloves	whole cloves

You can make these quick cookies out of almost any flavour jelly powder, but the red varieties look the best and generally speaking, taste the best too. This is a good cookie for the Christmas season. It adds colour to a plate of cookies. It is also very easy to make up a batch when the teacher sends home a note saying "Susie needs 2 dozen cookies for the class party tomorrow."

Mix together the condensed milk, the large pkg. of jelly powder, the coconut and the wafer crumbs. Roll approximately 1 tsp. (5 mL) of dough into a ball and then roll in additional jelly powder from the small package. Your hands will get progressively messier but you can scrape all the goo off at the end with a spoon and make the final sugar ball. Top each ball with a whole clove or a dash of green cherry as if to make a leaf. It is best not to use whole cloves if little kids are likely to be eating the cookies — (they sometimes forget to remove the thing and they get this funny look on their face.)

GOOEY BROWNIES

2 squares unsweetened chocolate, 1 oz. each	2 squares unsweetened chocolate, 28 g each
½ cup butter or margarine	125 mL butter or margarine
1 cup sugar	250 mL sugar
2 eggs	2 eggs
1 tsp. vanilla	5 mL vanilla
½ cup sifted flour	125 mL sifted flour
½ cup chopped walnuts*	125 mL chopped walnuts*

Melt the chocolate over hot water. Cream butter and sugar. Add eggs and beat well. Blend in the melted chocolate, vanilla and flour. Mix in nuts last. Pour into greased 8 x 8" (2 L) pan and bake in a 325°F (160°C) oven about 30 minutes. Be careful not to over bake. They are best on the gooey side.

*You can also use raisins or pecans instead of walnuts.

BARNEY GOOGLE SQUARES

1½ cups flour	375 mL flour
⅓ cup butter or margarine	75 mL butter or margarine
1 tsp. baking powder	5 mL baking powder
jam	jam
1 egg	1 egg
1 tbsp. milk	15 mL milk
½ cup butter or margarine, melted	125 mL butter or margarine, melted
½ cup sugar	125 mL sugar
½ tsp. vanilla	2 mL vanilla
2 cups coconut	500 mL coconut

Mix the flour, butter or margarine and baking powder as you would pastry — by cutting the shortening into the dry ingredients. Spread in an 8 x 8" (2 L) pan and cover with whatever jam is on the go at your house. We did it with cherry and it was lovely. Be as generous as you like.

Beat egg until light. Add the milk, melted butter or margarine, sugar, vanilla and coconut. Spread over the jam layer. Bake in a 350°F (180°C) oven for 30 minutes or until nicely browned.

In the 1930's, one of the Calgary radio stations offered a prize for the best new cake recipe.

Hundreds of recipes were submitted, and the judges chose the Barney Google Squares. Whether they chose it for its basic good taste or its original name, we're not sure. But we have to admit it sings in more ways than one!

andy was an enormous treat in the early days. It had to be a very special occasion before a woman would dip into her precious store of sugar and cocoa in order to make something so unredeemable as candy.

However, the kids in the household weren't so reluctant. I can remember my sisters making fudge — just for something to do on a cold winter's night. Also, Jim and I made toffee once when we were babysitting. I had read romantic tales of happy families happily working together to produce toffee and then happily "pulling" it together.

I must have thought we needed a shot of happiness for I made the toffee according to the instructions and then called in the other kids to help "pull" the stuff.

You've never seen such a mess. It never really pulled the way it was supposed to but it stuck . . . to our hands, arms, clothes, hair, the cupboard, the floor. Mom found remnants of it for weeks!

We have a recipe for toffee in the following section, but it's a no-nonsense thing that doesn't require pulling. We learned that particular sticky lesson!

PEANUT BUTTER BALLS

1 cup peanut butter	250 mL peanut butter
¼ cup liquid honey	50 mL liquid honey
¼ cup sesame seeds	50 mL sesame seeds
½ cup raisins	125 mL raisins
½ cup powdered skim milk	125 mL powdered skim milk

Mix all ingredients together. Roll into one inch balls. Refrigerate. Makes about 18. A great nutritious snack.

FANTASY FUDGE

3 cups sugar	750 mL sugar
¾ cup margarine	175 mL margarine
⅔ cup evaporated milk	150 mL evaporated milk
6 oz. pkg. semi-sweet chocolate chips	175 g pkg. semi-sweet chocolate chips
7 oz. jar marshmallow creme	198 g jar marshmallow creme
1 tsp. vanilla	5 mL vanilla
½ cup peanut butter	125 mL peanut butter

Combine 1½ cups (375 mL) sugar, 6 tbsp. (75 mL) margarine and ⅓ cup (75 mL) evaporated milk in heavy 1½ quart (1.5 L) saucepan; bring to a full rolling boil, stirring constantly. Continue boiling for 4 minutes over medium heat, stirring constantly. Remove from heat; stir in chocolate chips until melted. Add ½ jar of marshmallow creme and ½ tsp. (2 mL) vanilla. Beat until well blended.

Pour into greased 9 x 13" (3.5 L) pan. Repeat this process with remaining ingredients, substituting peanut butter for chocolate chips. Spread over chocolate layer. Cool at room temperature. Cut into squares.

SNOWBANK FUDGE

4 cups sugar	1 L sugar
10 level tbsp. cocoa	150 mL cocoa
4 tbsp. corn syrup	50 mL corn syrup
(white or dark)	(white or dark)
1⅓ cups milk	325 mL milk
2 tbsp. vanilla	25 mL vanilla
4 tbsp. butter	50 mL butter

In a heavy pot, mix together the sugar, cocoa, syrup and milk. Bring to a boil and keep to a rolling boil for 8 minutes on medium high heat. Don't stir.

At the 8 minute mark, test the syrup. It should be at the soft ball stage. In other words, if a drop of the hot mixture is dropped into a bowl of ice water, the drop will make a soft ball. You could also use a thermometer for this part of the process. The soft ball stage comes at 235°F (115°C).

Remove from heat and stir in the vanilla and butter. Now it is time to move out to the snowbank. Dawn, who makes this every Christmas takes the pan outside and sits it in a snowbank while she stirs away. It only takes a few minutes and leaves neat round holes in her backyard snowbanks.

If you haven't any snowbanks handy, use a bowl of icewater to help the mixture cool down. Stir while it's cooling until the mixture is sticky.

At this point, move back inside or remove the pan from the ice water and continue to beat energetically. The secret to this old fashioned brand of fudge is the beating.

When the mixture begins to lose its gloss and thicken up, then it is ready to pour into prepared greased pans. Let sit until hardened. Then cover and keep in the refrigerator or freeze.

CHOCOLATE FUDGE

4 cups sugar	1 L sugar
1 can (1 lb.) evaporated milk	454 g evaporated milk
½ cup margarine	125 mL margarine
12 oz. chocolate chips	350 g chocolate chips
2 squares unsweetened chocolate	2 squares unsweetened chocolate
1 jar (7 oz.) marshmallow creme	198 g marshmallow creme
1½ tsp. vanilla	7 mL vanilla
walnuts (optional)	walnuts (optional)

Combine the first three ingredients in a heavy large pot and bring to a boil. Boil for 6 minutes (a rolling boil). Remove from heat.

Add the chocolate chips, unsweetened chocolate, marshmallow creme and vanilla. Beat until everything is melted and blended in. Stir in nuts.

Pour into greased 9 x 13" (3.5 L) greased pan.

PUFFED WHEAT CANDY

⅓ cup butter or margarine	75 mL butter or margarine
½ cup corn syrup	125 mL corn syrup
1 cup brown sugar	250 mL brown sugar
2 tbsp. cocoa	30 mL cocoa
1 tsp. vanilla	5 mL vanilla
8 cups puffed wheat cereal	2 L puffed wheat cereal

Melt butter or margarine in a saucepan. Add the corn syrup, sugar, cocoa and vanilla. As soon as the mixture begins to bubble, remove from heat and pour over the puffed wheat. Mix as much as possible.

Put into a buttered pan about 9 x 13" (3.5 L) size. Press down well with buttered spoon or hands. Cut into squares.

CHEERIO BARS

½ cup butter or margarine	125 mL butter or margarine
3 cups miniature marshmallows (or 36 large)	750 mL miniature marshmallows (or 36 large)
½ cup peanut butter	125 mL peanut butter
½ cup nonfat dry milk powder	125 mL nonfat dry milk powder
¼ cup orange-flavoured breakfast drink powder	50 mL orange-flavoured breakfast drink powder
½-1 cup raisins	125-250 mL raisins
4 cups cheerio cereal	1 L cheerio cereal

In large saucepan, melt butter and marshmallows over low heat, stirring constantly. Stir in peanut butter until blended. Mix in milk and orange drink powder. Remove from heat, fold in raisins and cereal and stir until evenly coated. Pat into 9 x 9" (2.5 L) greased pan. Cool and cut into squares.

TOFFEE

2 cups sugar	500 mL sugar
¼ cup butter (no substitutes)	50 mL butter (no substitutes)
½ tsp. salt	2 mL salt
1½ cups white corn syrup	375 mL white corn syrup
1 tin (14 oz.) sweetened condensed milk	395 g sweetened condensed milk

In a large heavy pot, mix the ingredients. Bring to a boil over high heat. Stir constantly. If you don't, you will get brown flecks in the mixture. Turn heat to medium and continue boiling to the hard ball stage (250°F-150°C on your candy thermometer). If you haven't a thermometer, try dropping little drops of the boiling mixture into ice water. When one of the drops holds its shape but is still pliable, then you are close enough. It shouldn't be brittle.

Pour into buttered pans. Don't make the candy too thick. Use several pans, if necessary. Mark into squares before it cools.

As for cutting once it is cool, it's easiest to break it into pieces.

Pies

ANNUAL
BAZAAR

PIES
75¢

The Annual Bake Sale and Bazaar

Back row:
   Rhubarb Pie and Pumpkin Pie

Middle row:
   Flapper Pie
   Raspberry Pie To Dream On
   Yes Yogurt Pie

Front row:
   Cranberry Pie
   Blanche's Apple Pie
   Lemon Meringue Pie

Pies have been lost in the shuffle the last few years, the shuffle that has seen such splendours as cheesecake and Black Forest cake take over dessert supremacy.

Well, I would like to lead a pie liberation movement. They've been discriminated against and neglected too long. It's time they were returned to some of their former glory.

In Mom's time, a pie was a pie was a pie. Everybody made them — some better than others — but it was a respected and practical art form. Lard was cheap and readily available for the crusts. Fillings were made from wild berries and rhubarb in the summer; dried fruits, apples and custards in the winter.

Nobody fussed a lot over the process. The homemakers just made their routine pies over and over again until, without realizing it, they were making dessert masterpieces. Modern restaurants could build a reputation (and a good bank account) around some of the berry pies that were regularly turned out years ago!

On certain special occasions — like a community picnic — the women would trot out their specialties, like sour cream raisin or wild blueberry. Then the bachelors would quickly line up at the booth to get a piece of their favourite variety before it was all gone.

As far as I was concerned, the best pies were the berry pies. Nothing could beat a wild raspberry pie, all red and juicy, covered with a lattice crust . . . a sight for sore eyes and a treat for keen appetites. Karen would walk across hot coals for a lowbush cranberry pie laced with raisins, her all time favorite pie. Susan likes rhubarb and strawberry. Jim likes saskatoon. Ken, sensibly, likes them all.

In the early days, we very seldom added ice cream or whipped cream to the finished product. The pie had to stand or fall on its own flavour, and it always came through with flying colours.

There wasn't the same concern over a clean oven then either. Seems to me most ovens were a sensible black colour so that when pies ran over, they ran over. It was part of the process and eventually the oven would be scraped and swept out.

But to give you an idea of how the mighty have fallen, let me tell you about a pie encounter of the strange kind.

I ordered a piece of raisin pie in a restaurant en route to the Peace River country recently. My kids ordered pizza. When I got the pie, I was puzzled by a taste I couldn't quite identify. Whatever it was, it didn't taste at all like raisin pie should taste. Finally, I twigged to the fact that the crust of this so-called pie was made of the same dough that the pizzas were made from.

Raisin pie with pizza pastry. Is there nothing sacred?

Pie making is not an inherited talent, however. Like many other skills it has to be learned, as Karen found out in her batching days.

One of her roommates offered to make a pie with the saskatoons they had picked the day before at Saskatoon Lake, naturally. By the way, she said to Karen, how do you make a saskatoon pie?

You make the crust, Karen said, and then make the filling and then top it with more crust. Easy, she said.

OK, her roommate said.

It was a rather flat looking pie when it was finished, Karen noticed, but then looks aren't everything so she said nothing until the first course was finished. On came the pie.

Her roommate had taken her instructions literally. She had made a bottom crust, covered it with one layer of saskatoons and then covered it all with another layer of pastry. No sugar to sweeten the berries, no flour to bind them together. Just berries and two crusts.

When the pie was cut and served, all the berries naturally ran out of the enclosing pastry, leaving two flat pieces of pastry and a pile of dry hard berries.

It was one of your basic unforgettable moments and her roommate still gets teased. She's since learned to make very good pies and Karen has learned to give more complete instructions!

One last word about pies. Our cousin Leif came from Denmark one year to live with us and learn about Canada. Naturally he learned first how to swear and how to drive the tractor too fast — which kept Mom in a constant state of annoyance — but he also learned to love Mom's pies — which counteracted some of his other learned behaviours. When he went back to the old country, he took along a pie recipe and gave it first to his Mom and later to his wife. Neither could quite come up with a Canadian pie, he tells us, and he still misses them.

Your pies are special, he says.

We should pay attention.

In the following section, we have something old and something new, a few borrowed recipes and even a few that are blue.

Read, eat and enjoy!

PIE CRUST

5 cups flour	1.25 L flour
4 tbsp. brown sugar	50 mL brown sugar
½ tsp. baking soda	2 mL baking soda
dash of salt	dash of salt
1 lb. lard	500 g lard
1 egg	1 egg
water	water
1 tbsp. vinegar	15 mL vinegar

Mix the flour, brown sugar, soda and salt together in a fairly large bowl. Cut in the lard (with pastry blender or fingers) until the mixture is crumbly.

In a measuring cup, beat the egg slightly and add water to make ¾ cup (175 mL) liquid. Add the vinegar and mix slightly. Add to the flour mixture and stir until mixed. Hands are most effective in making this pie dough — and most other pie doughs, for that matter!

Keep in a plastic bag in the freezer. Whenever you need some, let the dough thaw, use whatever is necessary and then refreeze. This stuff is a bear for punishment — it takes freezing and thawing and beating about and still comes out flaky and tasty.

Warm handed people have to take care, however. Sometimes in working the lard into the flour, the lards gets soft too quickly and the whole thing turns into a sticky ball. A light hand is the secret.

CRANBERRY PIE

pie dough for bottom crust and lattice top	pie dough for bottom crust and lattice top
3 cups cranberries, frozen or fresh	750 mL cranberries, frozen or fresh
1 cup raisins	250 mL raisins
1½ cups sugar	375 mL sugar
4 tbsp. minute tapioca*	50 mL minute tapioca*
1 egg	1 egg

Mix the cranberries, raisins, sugar, tapioca and egg. Let stand while rolling out the bottom crust. Fill the crust and finish with a lattice type arrangement. Bake in 400°F (200°C) oven for 15 minutes; then reduce heat and bake about 30 minutes at 350°F (180°C).

Expect the pie to spill over the edges — it's not a prize winner unless it does. Therefore, use a pie shield or put some foil under the drips.

*Substitute 3 tbsp. (50 mL) flour.

FRESH FRUIT PIES

Summer pies allow plenty of scope for creativity! You can use strawberries, raspberries, blueberries, cherries, rhubarb, saskatoon and various combinations. The amount of sugar and thickener will depend on the tartness and degree of ripeness of the fruit. Also, the amount of thickener you want to use (flour, minute tapioca or cornstarch) depends to a large degree on the firmness you prefer in a pie filling.

For a 9" (23 cm) pie, the usual proportion of fruit to sugar and thickener is as follows:

4 cups fresh fruit	1 L fresh fruit
1 cup sugar	250 mL sugar
3-4 tbsp. flour	50 mL flour
flavouring*	flavouring*
1-2 tbsp. butter	15-25 mL butter

Prepare and roll out pastry for bottom crust. Adjust in the pie plate.

Combine the sugar and flour. Mix lightly with the fruit and flavouring, and fill the pie plate. Dot with butter. Place top pastry over the filling, or arrange a lattice crust so that the colour of the bright summer berries shows through.

Bake at 425ºF (220ºC) for 10-15 minutes; reduce heat to 375ºF (190ºC) and bake for 30 minutes or until done.

*The flavouring used may include almond extract, lemon juice, cinnamon . . . whatever strikes your fancy!

RHUBARB CUSTARD PIE

pastry for a 9" pie	pastry for a 23 cm pie
3 cups rhubarb, cut into chunks	750 mL rhubarb, cut into chunks
1½ cups sugar	375 mL sugar
3 tbsp. flour	50 mL flour
½ tsp. nutmeg	2 mL nutmeg
2 eggs, well beaten	2 eggs, well beaten
2 tbsp. cream	25 mL cream
1 tbsp. butter or margarine	15 mL butter or margarine

Line the pie plate with pastry. Place the cut-up rhubarb in the shell.

Combine the sugar, flour, nutmeg. Beat eggs and cream. Add dry ingredients. Mix well and pour over the rhubarb. Dot with butter or margarine.

Cover with a lattice crust — that is strips of woven crust. Bake at 450ºF (230ºC) for 10 minutes; then reduce heat to 350ºF (180ºC) and bake 30 minutes or until crust is brown and rhubarb tender.

RHUBARB SUMMER PIE

pie crust for single crust pie	pie crust for single crust pie
½ cup sour cream	125 mL sour cream
½ cup cooked rhubarb	125 mL cooked rhubarb
½ cup raisins	125 mL raisins
1 cup sugar	250 mL sugar
1 tsp. cinnamon	5 mL cinnamon
¼ tsp. cloves	1 mL cloves
1 tbsp. flour	15 mL flour
3 eggs, separated	3 eggs, separated
⅓ cup sugar	75 mL sugar

Mix the sour cream with the cooked rhubarb. Add the raisins. Mix the sugar, flour and spices together; add to the rhubarb mixture. Beat the egg yolks and add.

Pour into a pastry lined pie plate and bake at 350°F (180°C) until the filling is set and the crust well baked — about 30-35 minutes.

When the pie has cooked, beat the egg whites until they stand in peaks. Continue beating and slowly add the ⅓ cup (75 mL) sugar until the mixture is thick and glossy. Heap lightly over the pie and brown in a 350°F (180°C) oven about 10 minutes or until the meringue is just right.

STRAWBERRY RHUBARB CHIFFON PIE

flapper pie crust, page 166	flapper pie crust, page 166
2 cups rhubarb, cut in chunks (fresh or frozen)	500 mL rhubarb, cut in chunks (fresh or frozen)
2 tbsp. sugar	30 mL sugar
¼ cup water	50 mL water
1 pkg. (3 oz.) strawberry flavoured jelly powder	1 pkg. (85 g) strawberry flavoured jelly powder
1 pkg. (10 oz.) frozen strawberries sweetened	1 pkg. (285 g) frozen strawberries sweetened
½ cup whipping cream	125 mL whipping cream

Line a 9" (23 cm) pie plate with flapper pie crust and bake until lightly browned. Cool.

Combine rhubarb, sugar and water in a saucepan. Simmer uncovered 5-10 minutes or until rhubarb can be broken with a fork, and is tender. Remove from heat and add the jelly powder, stirring until completely dissolved. Add frozen block of strawberries and stir until berries are separated. Chill until slightly thickened.

When the fruit mixture begins to thicken, whip the cream until stiff. Fold into the fruit mixture. Pour into the cooled pie shell and chill about 3 hours.

Garnish with additional whipped cream if you are up to it.

LEMON MERINGUE PIE

one baked 9" pie shell	one baked 23 cm pie shell
1½ cups sugar	375 mL sugar
7 tbsp. cornstarch	100 mL cornstarch
1½ cups water	375 mL water
3 egg yolks, slightly beaten	3 egg yolks, slightly beaten
3 tbsp. butter	50 mL butter
6 tbsp. lemon juice	75 mL lemon juice
2 tbsp. grated lemon rind	30 mL grated lemon rind

In a medium sized saucepan, mix together the sugar, cornstarch and water. Slowly bring to a boil and stir constantly for about 5 minutes until the mixture is thick and clear. Remove from the heat and stir a bit of the mixture into the beaten egg yolks. Then add all of the egg yolk mixture back into the sugar mixture and return to the heat, stirring constantly over low heat for another 5 minutes or so until the mixture is once again thick and smooth. Remove from heat. Add the butter, lemon juice and grated rind. Pour into baked pie shell.

MERINGUE

3 egg whites	3 egg whites
¼ tsp. cream of tartar	1 mL cream of tartar
6 tbsp. sugar	75 mL sugar
½ tsp. vanilla	2 mL vanilla

Beat egg whites and cream of tartar until stiff. Add sugar gradually, beating all the while until the egg whites are glossy and stand in firm peaks. Add vanilla.

Spread meringue right out to the edges of the filling so that the meringue won't shrink away from the sides. Bake at 350°F (180°C) for 12-15 minutes or until lightly browned.

LEMON PIE WITH A TWIST

pastry for 2 crust 9" pie	pastry for 2 crust 23 cm pie
2 medium lemons	2 medium lemons
1½ cups sugar	375 mL sugar
4 eggs	4 eggs

The day before you want to serve this pie, cut the lemons into paper thin slices, discarding seeds as you work. Put into a medium sized bowl and sprinkle the sugar on top. Gently stir; cover and let stand at room temperature overnight.

The next day, prepare the pastry and line the bottom of a pie plate.

Beat the eggs slightly with a fork or whisk and then gently fold into the lemon mixture. Mix gently just to be sure the sugar is completely dissolved. Pour into the pastry lined pie plate. Cover with top pastry layer — trim or add cut-outs or simply allow slits for the escape of steam.

Bake at 425°F (220°C) for 15 minutes; then reduce temperature to 350°F (180°C) and continue baking about 30 minutes until crust is golden and knife inserted in centre comes out clean. Serve warm or cold. Servings may be small because this is very tart, almost bitter, but very very good.

BLANCHE'S APPLE PIE

pastry for a two-crust 9" pie
6 or 7 tart apples
¾-1 cup sugar
  (depends on tartness of apples)
2 tbsp. flour
1 tsp. cinnamon
dash of salt
2 tbsp. butter

pastry for a two-crust 23 cm pie
6 or 7 tart apples
175-250 mL sugar
  (depends on tartness of apples)
30 mL flour
5 mL cinnamon
dash of salt
25 mL butter

Pare apples and slice thin. Combine the sugar, flour and cinnamon and mix with the apples. Line a 9" (23 cm) pie plate with pastry; fill with the apple mixture and dot with butter.

Roll out the top crust and before putting it on the pie, cut out a fern leaf or violin design. Then adjust on the top of the pie and seal the edges. Sprinkle with sugar for sparkle or brush the top with cream to get a golden finish.

Bake in 400°F (200°C) oven for 50 minutes or until done. Check the apples with a fork — they should be soft and bubbling.

Serve with ice cream, whipped cream or cheddar cheese.

APPLE CRANBERRY RAISIN PIE

pastry for 9" two crust pie
1 cup cranberries*
1 cup sugar
½ cup raisins
3 tbsp. flour
dash of salt
peel of 1 lemon
5 cooking apples, peeled, sliced
2 tbsp. butter

pastry for 23 cm two crust pie
250 mL cranberries*
250 mL sugar
125 mL raisins
50 mL flour
dash of salt
peel of 1 lemon
5 cooking apples, peeled, sliced
25 mL butter

In a large bowl, combine the cranberries, sugar, raisins, flour, salt and lemon peel. Add apples and mix well.

Place in a pastry lined pie plate and dot with butter. Cut generous vents into the top crust and arrange over the fruit. Seal edges well, but expect drips nevertheless. Use a pie shield or strategically placed pieces of foil in the oven.

Bake in 425°F (220°C) oven for 10 minutes. Then reduce heat to 350°F (180°C) and bake another 30-40 minutes, just until the apples are tender and the crust is browned.

*Canned cranberry sauce can be used. Cut down on the sugar if you do so.

SOUR CREAM RAISIN PIE

1 baked 9" pie shell	1 baked 23 cm pie shell
1 cup brown sugar	250 mL brown sugar
2 tbsp. flour	30 mL flour
¼ tsp. cinnamon	1 mL cinnamon
pinch of cloves	pinch of cloves
pinch of salt	pinch of salt
3 egg yolks	3 egg yolks
2 cups sour cream	500 mL sour cream
2 tbsp. milk	25 mL milk
1 cup raisins	250 mL raisins
1 cup heavy cream, whipped	250 mL heavy cream, whipped

Combine sugar, flour, spices and salt in heavy saucepan. Beat egg yolks. Add sour cream and milk, beating until well blended. Add egg yolk mixture and raisins to sugar mixture. Bring to boil over medium heat; boil for 2 minutes continuing to stir. Remove from heat; let cool for ten minutes.

Turn into pie crust. Refrigerate for 3 hours or overnight. Spread whipped cream over filling.

HOT RAISIN SOUR CREAM PIE

one baked 9" pie shell	one baked 23 cm pie shell
2 cups raisins	500 mL raisins
1 cup water	250 mL water
2 cups sour cream	500 ml sour cream
3 egg yolks	3 egg yolks
1 tbsp. flour	15 mL flour
⅓ cup sugar	75 mL sugar
½ tsp. cinnamon	2 mL cinnamon
¼ tsp. nutmeg	1 mL nutmeg
3 egg whites	3 egg whites
2 tbsp. sugar	30 mL sugar

Prepare the pie shell, bake and cool.

Simmer the raisins in the water until most of the water is gone. Set aside to cool.

Mix together the sour cream, egg yolks, flour, sugar, and spices and add to the raisins. Cook over low heat until thick and smooth. Pour into prepared pie shell.

Whip the egg whites until they hold soft peaks. Slowly add the sugar and continue beating until stiff peaks form. Spread over the pie being sure to cover right to the edges.

Bake in a 325°F (160°C) oven for about 10 minutes or until meringue peaks get ever-so-slightly brown.

RAISIN PIE

pastry for two crust pie	pastry for two crust pie
1 cup brown sugar	250 mL brown sugar
2½ tbsp. flour	40 mL flour
¼ tsp. salt	1 mL salt
1½ cups cold water	375 mL cold water
1½ cups raisins	375 mL raisins
3 tbsp. lemon juice	50 mL lemon juice
1 tbsp. butter	15 mL butter

Mix the sugar, flour, salt, water and raisins in a medium sized saucepan. Cook over medium heat until the mixture thickens and clarifies. Remove from heat and add the butter and lemon juice.

Bake between two crusts for 30-40 minutes, or until the pastry seems well cooked.

PUMPKIN PIE

pastry for 9" single crust pie	pastry for 23 cm single crust pie
2 cups cooked or canned pumpkin*	500 mL cooked or canned pumpkin*
1 cup milk	250 mL milk
3 eggs, separated	3 eggs, separated
1 cup sugar	250 mL sugar
½ tsp. cinnamon	2 mL cinnamon
¼ tsp. cloves	1 mL cloves
¼ tsp. nutmeg	1 mL nutmeg

Prepare the pastry and line the pie plate. This recipe makes a lot of filling so when you line the pie plate, leave a high narrow edge on the dough.

In a large bowl, mix the pumpkin and milk. Then beat the egg yolks well and add to the pumpkin mixture. Mix the sugar with the spices and add to the pumpkin. Finally, beat the egg whites until stiff and fold into the pumpkin mixture.

Put the empty pie shell into the oven and bring the filling to it. Pour the filling into the pie shell.

Bake about 45 minutes in a 350°F (180°C) oven until done, or until a knife inserted in the centre comes out clean.

Serve with real whipped cream. Pumpkin pie calls for it; yea, deserves it.

*This pie is also very good with cooked mashed carrots in place of the pumpkin.

MOCK CHERRY PIE

pastry for 9" pie plus lattice strips	pastry for 23 cm pie plus lattice strips
1¾ cups sugar	425 mL sugar
2 tbsp. cornstarch	30 mL cornstarch
¼ tsp. salt	1 mL salt
¾ cup water	175 mL water
3 cups fresh or frozen cranberries	750 mL fresh or frozen cranberries
2 tbsp. butter	25 mL butter
½ tsp. almond extract	2 mL almond extract

In a medium saucepan, combine sugar, cornstarch and salt. Add the water and bring to a boil. Add the cranberries and cook for 5-8 minutes or until the berries have popped. Stir often. Add butter and almond extract.

Turn into pastry lined pie plate. Cover with a lattice top. Bake at 400°F (200°C) for about half an hour, or until crust is nicely browned and the filling bubbly.

VANILLA CREAM PIE

one baked 9" pie shell	one baked 23 cm pie shell
½ cup flour	125 mL flour
½ cup sugar	125 mL sugar
¼ tsp. salt	1 mL salt
3 cups milk	750 mL milk
3 egg yolks, slightly beaten	3 egg yolks, slightly beaten
1½ tsp. vanilla	7 mL vanilla
1 tbsp. butter	15 mL butter

Combine the flour, sugar and salt in a medium saucepan. Add milk gradually, stirring until smooth. Cook over medium heat, stirring constantly until mixture thickens. Beat egg yolks and add to the milk mixture, stirring until smooth. Cook for 2 minutes longer. Remove from heat. Stir in vanilla and butter. Cool slightly. Cover with waxed paper to prevent skin forming.

Turn cooled filling into pie shell. Top with meringue or whipped cream, if desired.

COCONUT CREAM PIE

Prepare Vanilla Cream pie as directed above. Add ¾ cup (175 mL) coconut to cooked filling. Sprinkle meringue with more coconut before baking or sprinkle over whipped cream topping.

BANANA CREAM PIE

Prepare Vanilla Cream pie as directed above. Slice 2 small bananas over bottom of a baked pie shell before adding cooled filling. Garnish with additional banana slices if using the whipped cream topping.

CHOCOLATE CREAM PIE

one baked 9" pastry shell	one baked 23 cm pastry shell
½ cup cocoa	125 mL cocoa
¾ cup sugar	175 mL sugar
⅓ cup flour*	75 mL flour*
¼ tsp. salt	1 mL salt
2 cups milk	500 mL milk
3 egg yolks, slightly beaten	3 egg yolks, slightly beaten
2 tbsp. butter or margarine	25 mL butter or margarine
1 tsp. vanilla	5 mL vanilla
3 egg whites	3 egg whites
2 tbsp. sugar	30 mL sugar

In heavy saucepan or double boiler, combine cocoa, sugar, flour and salt. Gradually stir in the milk. Cook and stir over medium heat until mixture boils and thickens. Add beaten egg yolks and cook for 2 minutes longer. Remove from heat. Add butter or margarine and vanilla. Cool to room temperature and pour into baked pie shell.

Top with meringue. Beat egg whites until stiff. Slowly add sugar. Spread on pie.

*If you prefer, you can use 3 tbsp. cornstarch in place of the flour.

BANANA BUTTERSCOTCH PIE

one baked 9" pie shell	one baked 23 cm pie shell
1 cup brown sugar	250 mL brown sugar
⅓ cup flour	75 mL flour
3 tbsp. butter	50 mL butter
dash of salt	dash of salt
2 cups scalded milk	500 mL scalded milk
2 eggs	2 eggs
½ tsp. vanilla	2 mL vanilla
bananas	bananas

Prepare and bake the pie shell. Let cool while making the filling.

In a double boiler, combine the brown sugar, flour, butter and salt. Put over boiling water and cook together until well blended.

Scald the milk in another pot and add to the brown sugar mixture. Stir furiously until the mixture thickens. Try to prevent lumps. Beat the eggs until light. Put a little of the milk mixture into the eggs and then return it all to the double boiler. Stir again until the mixture is thick and smooth. Remove from heat and add the vanilla. Stir until the custard cools slightly.

Slice 1-2 bananas over the bottom of the pie shell. Save some for garnish. Cover with the butterscotch mixture. Let cool and serve with whipped cream and more bananas.

FLAPPER PIE

7 double graham wafers, crushed
  (about 1½ cups)
½ cup sugar
½ tsp. cinnamon
¼ cup melted butter or margarine
2 cups milk
3 tbsp. cornstarch
¼ cup sugar
2 eggs, separated
1 tsp. vanilla
2 tbsp. sugar

7 double graham wafers, crushed
  (about 375 mL)
125 mL sugar
2 mL cinnamon
50 mL melted butter or margarine
500 mL milk
50 mL cornstarch
50 mL sugar
2 eggs, separated
5 mL vanilla
30 mL sugar

Crush the graham wafers and add the sugar, cinnamon and melted butter or margarine. Reserve ⅓ cup (75 mL). Press what is left into a pie plate, across the bottom and up the sides to the edge of the plate. Bake in 325°F (160°C) oven for 15 minutes, just long enough for the wafers to stick together and brown slightly.

Mix the milk, cornstarch and sugar in a medium saucepan. Place over medium heat, stirring constantly until the mixture thickens. If you don't stir constantly, you will get interesting little brown spots in the mixture. If that happens, there is no harm. If just doesn't look as nice so stir to avoid it.

Separate the eggs and beat the yolks well. Add some of the hot milk mixture to the egg yolks, then put them all back into the hot milk mixture. Stir, over medium heat, until thick and smooth. Remove from heat, add the vanilla and cool slightly. Pour into the graham wafer crust.

Beat the egg whites until stiff peaks form. Add the 2 tbsp. (30 mL) sugar gradually, beating well. Cover the custard layer with the egg white meringue. Top with reserved crumbs. Bake until meringue browns — about 5 minutes at 400°F (200°C). Cool until completely set — a good 4-5 hours.

COTTAGE CHEESE PIE

one unbaked 9" pie shell
1½ cups creamed cottage cheese
3 eggs, separated
¾ cup sugar
2 tbsp. flour
1 tbsp. butter, melted
¼ cup currants or raisins
½ tsp. vanilla
½ tsp. grated lemon rind

one unbaked 23 cm pie shell
375 mL creamed cottage cheese
3 eggs, separated
175 mL sugar
30 mL flour
15 mL butter, melted
50 mL currants or raisins
2 mL vanilla
2 mL grated lemon rind

Mash the cottage cheese through a sieve or whirl in a blender for a few minutes in order to get a smooth texture.

Beat the egg yolks and add sugar, flour and melted butter. Mix well. Add the mashed cottage cheese, currants or raisins, vanilla and lemon rind. Beat the egg whites until stiff and fold into the cheese mixture.

Pour the mixture into a pie plate lined with pastry. Bake in a 325°F (160°C) oven for 40 minutes or until the filling is set and the crust is well baked.

Custard pies like this one tend to result in soggy bottom crusts. To prevent that, brush the unbaked crust with unbeaten egg white before pouring in the cheese mixture. Take a bit from the egg white mixture before it gets beaten, or use another egg.

RASPBERRY PIE TO DREAM ON

PASTRY:

¼ cup butter	50 mL butter
dash of salt	dash of salt
2 tbsp. sugar	30 mL sugar
1 egg yolk	1 egg yolk
¾ cup flour	175 mL flour
¼ cup finely chopped almonds	50 mL finely chopped almonds

RASPBERRY FILLING:

10-12 oz. pkg. frozen raspberries	285-375 g frozen raspberries
1 cup sugar	250 mL sugar
2 egg whites, room temp.	2 egg whites, room temp.
1 tbsp. lemon juice	15 mL lemon juice
dash of salt	dash of salt
1 cup whipping cream, whipped	250 mL whipping cream, whipped
½ tsp. almond extract	2 mL almond extract

To make the pastry shell, cream the butter, salt and sugar until creamy and light. Add the egg yolk and beat well. Gradually add the flour and chopped almonds to make a firm dough. Press into a 9" (23 cm) pie plate and chill for 30 minutes. Then bake in a 400°F (200°C) oven for 15 minutes or until the shell is lightly browned.

To make the filling, thaw the raspberries (or if it's summer and you should be so lucky, pick them off your bushes . . . about 2 cups (500 mL) worth). Combine the raspberries, sugar, egg whites, lemon juice and salt. Beat for 15 minutes, beginning with a slow speed on the electric mixer and working up to faster speeds. Beat for at least 15 minutes. Fold in the whipped cream and almond extract. Mound into baked and cooled shell. Freeze until firm.

DUTCH PRUNE CHEESE PIE

one unbaked 9" pie shell	one unbaked 23 cm pie shell
1 cup chopped cooked prunes	250 mL chopped cooked prunes
⅓ cup sugar	75 mL sugar
2 tbsp. flour	30 mL flour
2 tsp. lemon juice	10 mL lemon juice
2 cups cottage cheese	500 mL cottage cheese
2 eggs	2 eggs
½ cup sugar	125 mL sugar
¼ cup cream	50 mL cream
2 tbsp. flour	30 mL flour
1 tsp. grated lemon rind	5 mL grated lemon rind
1 tbsp. lemon juice	15 mL lemon juice

Drain the prunes. Mix together the prunes, sugar, 2 tbsp. (30 mL) flour and 2 tsp. (10 mL) lemon juice. Spread evenly over the bottom of the pie shell.

Beat cottage cheese until smooth. Add eggs one at a time beating well after each addition. Add remaining ingredients and beat until filling is completely smooth. (The blender works well for this stage.)

Pour over the prune layer. Bake in a 350°F (180°C) oven for 1 hour or until set. Cool on rack and chill before serving.

YES YOGURT PIE

1½ cups vanilla wafer crumbs	375 mL vanilla wafer crumbs
¼ cup melted butter	50 mL melted butter
2 pkgs. unflavoured gelatin (7 g each)	2 pkgs. unflavoured gelatin (7 g each)
½ cup sugar	125 mL sugar
1 cup water	250 mL water
2 cups yogurt	500 mL yogurt
1 — 6 oz. can frozen orange juice concentrate	178 mL can frozen orange juice concentrate
2 egg whites	2 egg whites
2 tbsp. sugar	30 mL sugar
toasted coconut	toasted coconut

Combine the crumbs and melted butter. Press into pie plate, building up a solid rim. Chill while making the rest of the pie.

In small saucepan, combine the gelatin, sugar and water. Cook over low heat until gelatin and sugar are completely dissolved.

In another bowl, mix the yogurt and orange juice concentrate. Add the gelatine mixture.

Beat the egg whites until stiff peaks form and add 2 tbsp. (30 mL) sugar gradually, beating all the while. Fold the meringue gradually into the orange mixture. Chill until the mixture mounds when dropped from a spoon. Pour into prepared pie crust. Top with toasted coconut. Chill until firm.

HARRY'S BUTTER TARTS

4 eggs	4 eggs
4 tbsp. melted butter	50 mL melted butter
2 cups brown sugar	500 mL brown sugar
1 tsp. vanilla or lemon extract	5 mL vanilla or lemon extract
4 tbsp. cream	50 mL cream
2 cups currants or raisins	500 mL currants or raisins

Whip the eggs, butter, sugar and vanilla until cream coloured. Add cream and currants or raisins and pour into unbaked tart shells.

Bake in 400°F (200°C) oven for 5 minutes. Reduce heat to 375°F (190°C) and bake for about 12 minutes longer. Makes about 25 large tarts.

BUTTER TART SQUARES

1½ cups flour	375 mL flour
½ cup butter (softened)	125 mL butter (softened)
⅓ cup brown sugar	75 mL brown sugar

Mix ingredients and press into a 9 x 13" (3.5 L) pan. Bake at 350°F (180°C) for 15 minutes.

TOPPING:

½ cup butter	125 mL butter
2 tbsp. cream	25 mL cream
1 tsp. vanilla	5 mL vanilla
1 cup raisins or currants	250 mL raisins or currants
½ cup walnuts (optional)	125 mL walnuts (optional)
1 cup brown sugar	250 mL brown sugar
2 eggs	2 eggs
2 tbsp. flour	30 mL flour

Mix and spread over base. Return to oven and bake 20-30 minutes at 350°F (180°C) or until golden brown.

RED AND GREEN PIE

one baked 9" pie shell
2 envelopes unflavoured gelatin
   (7 g each)
½ cup cold water
1 can (6 oz.) frozen limeade
   concentrate
¼ cup sugar
¾ cup water
1 tsp. grated lime rind
   (optional)
1 cup diced strawberries
1 cup whipped cream
green food colouring

one baked 23 cm pie shell
2 envelopes unflavoured gelatin
   (7 g each)
125 mL cold water
178 mL frozen limeade
   concentrate
50 mL sugar
175 mL water
5 mL grated lime rind
   (optional)
250 mL diced strawberries
250 mL whipped cream
green food colouring

Soften the gelatin in ½ cup (125 mL) cold water.

In a small saucepan, combine the limeade concentrate, sugar and ¾ cup (175 mL) water. Cook until the sugar dissolves. Add the gelatin mixture and stir until dissolved. Chill until slightly set, then stir in the lime rind and strawberries. Whip the cream until stiff and fold into the lime mixture. Add enough green food colouring to colour everything a spring green. Chill once again until the mixture holds some shape but isn't completely set. Spoon into the pie shell and chill yet again.

The reason for the second chilling stage is to be able to mound the mixture into the pie shell. If you don't want mounds and want to cut out one step, put the mixture directly into the cooked pie shell and chill one final time. Garnish with more strawberries.

LEMON CHEESE

juice and rind of 3 medium lemons
2 cups sugar
½ cup butter
7 eggs, well beaten

juice and rind of 3 medium lemons
500 mL sugar
125 mL butter
7 eggs, well beaten

Mix lemon juice, sugar and butter in a double boiler. Add well beaten eggs and cook until thick, beating the mixture constantly with a wire whisk. Add the grated rind of lemons. Cool completely.

Use in tarts, as a cake filling or as jam. However this lemon cheese is used, it's light and very refreshing.

Preserves

Summer's Bounty

Autumn Relish
Dill Pickles
Sauerkraut Made in Jars
Beet Pickles
Pickled Zucchini
Mustard Pickles
High Bush Cranberry Jelly
Onion and Cucumber Relish
Rhubarb and Raspberry Jam
Rhubarb Relish

Homemakers in the early days worried so much about the future that they sometimes skimped on the present. That was never more evident in our household than at canning or freezing time.

We would have a few, very precious, feeds of new peas. The rest of the peas out there in the garden just seemed to disappear without a word of farewell.

One raspberry pie would go by us, leaving us hungering for another, but the other raspberries on the bushes seemed to vanish overnight.

It was all very frustrating but not particularly mysterious if we stopped to think for a minute. The peas and the raspberries and all the other wonders of summer were disappearing into quart jars or freezer packages . . . to be reborn in the depths of winter.

Women who lived through homesteading days, the depression and then wartime rationing naturally developed this habit of saving, of putting something away for a rainy day. Their talents are not that popular these days but if the economy continues its downward spiral, they may come back into style!

So, preserving was a very important element of housekeeping years ago because it ensured a food supply through the winter months.

It was also very important to the women because it was a tangible measure of their achievement. There was nothing to beat the feeling of accomplishment after canning a dozen quarts of raspberries, say, and seeing them sit on the cupboard with the sun shining through them like so many jars of jewels.

There's a great satisfaction in being able to say . . . I did that. I picked those, cleaned them, canned them. I did it.

And there's also great satisfaction in being able to tell the neighbour lady, "I have 100 quarts of saskatoons this year. How many have you?"

Competition was keen, believe me!

Once the jars had cooled and Mom had tightened the seal and labelled them, they were put down into the cellar.

I occasionally give away my not-so-tender years by asking one of my kids to go to the cellar for something. They, poor things, have no idea what a cellar is.

Many of us who grew up with them wished very sincerely that we knew nothing of them either. But we knew only too well . . . they were holes in the ground that were dark, scary, full of spiders and mice and other unspeakables.

Ours had shelves along two sides to hold jars and milk pails and the like. The end was made up of three bins — one for potatoes, one for carrots and one for miscellaneous like onions, turnips and so on. The fourth side was taken up with the steps leading down from the kitchen.

There was never a light down there, of course, and inevitably, the flashlight was broken or lost, so whatever had to be found had to be found by the weak light from above. And by feel.

Get potatoes, Mom would say to me. So I'd go down and hope very fervently that I could pick out ten potatoes without sticking my finger into a rotten one.

Or Mom would ask for a jar of currant jelly. I'd pick what I hoped was the right jelly and then shoot back up the stairs. But it would be saskatoon or crabapple or something so I'd have to creep down again . . . and again.

In the meantime, Jim would realize I was in the midst of my least favourite activity — cellar prowling — so he'd wait until just the right moment and close the trap door on me.

Then I'd holler and Mom would get disgusted with both of us. And so on it went, with endless variations. Someone should write a research paper on the effects of dark cellars on impressionable young girls.

But it spite of all that, the cellar was absolutely essential to our existence just as the garden had been months earlier.

Actually, there was more than one way to preserve foods, even before the freezer was happily invented. There was always the method of drying foods, and some ingenious homesteaders perfected that art too.

Mrs. M. Hitz tells about her grandmother who used to dry saskatoons. She would lie them on white sheets in the sun during the day and then bring them all in before the evening dews fell. Then she'd put them back out the next morning . . . and so on . . . until the berries were dry and could be stored in 100 pound flour sacks.

In the middle of winter, she'd take out enough berries for a meal, soak them overnight and then cook them up in pies or puddings as if they were fresh.

Our recipes in this section include some of the old favourites as well as some wild and wonderful new ideas. Read, Eat and Enjoy!

BASIC RHUBARB JAM

7 cups rhubarb	1.75 L rhubarb
4 cups sugar	1 L sugar
2 lemons, juice and rind	2 lemons, juice and rind
1 cup crushed pineapple with juice	250 mL crushed pineapple with juice

Clean the rhubarb and cut into ½" (1 cm) chunks. Put into a large heavy saucepan or a preserving kettle. Add the sugar, lemon juice and rind and pineapple.

Bring slowly to a boil and cook over low heat, stirring continually, until the mixture is thick and clear.

Pour into hot sterilized jars and seal.

This is a very basic recipe with all sorts of possibilities for variations. Instead of the pineapple, try adding 1 cup finely diced banana just before pouring into the jars. Or add saskatoons or strawberries in season.

Rhubarb is good as a base for many jam combinations. It's hard to go wrong.

RHUBARB JAM . . . vintage 1980's

5 cups rhubarb, cut fine	1.25 L rhubarb, cut fine
4 cups sugar	1 L sugar
1 pkg. (6 oz.) strawberry jelly powder	1 pkg. (170 g) strawberry jelly powder

Combine the rhubarb and sugar and let sit for a few minutes until juice begins to form. Then put it on the heat and cook until the rhubarb is tender. Add strawberry jelly powder and cook and stir until the powder is thoroughly dissolved.

Pour into hot sterilized jars and seal.

RHUBARB AND RASPBERRY JAM

4 cups rhubarb, diced	1 L rhubarb, diced
2 cups red raspberries	500 mL red raspberries
4 cups sugar	1 L sugar

Wash and cut the rhubarb into ½" (1.5 cm) pieces.

Clean the raspberries and add to the rhubarb. Add the sugar and stir gently. Let stand several hours until some of the juice is extracted. Then put into a large heavy saucepan or a preserving kettle and boil rapidly until the jam is thick.

Pour into hot sterile jars and seal.

SASKATOON AND RHUBARB JAM

4 cups rhubarb, diced	1 L rhubarb, diced
½ cup water	125 mL water
6 cups saskatoons	1.5 L saskatoons
6 cups sugar	1.5 L sugar

Boil the rhubarb with the water until the rhubarb is soft. Put the saskatoons through a food chopper and mix in with the sugar and rhubarb. Boil 10 minutes.

Pour into hot sterile jars and seal.

SASKATOON PIE FILLING

4 cups water	1 L water
¾ cup lemon juice	175 mL lemon juice
10 cups saskatoons, frozen or fresh	2.5 L saskatoons, frozen or fresh
3 cups sugar	750 mL sugar
1 cup cornstarch	250 mL cornstarch

Bring the water and lemon juice to a boil. Then add the saskatoons and just bring to a boil again. Remove from heat.

Mix well the sugar and cornstarch. Add to berries and stir until juice is clear. Seal in jars while hot. This method can be used for canning blueberries as well.

HIGH BUSH CRANBERRY JELLY

Find and pick some high bush cranberries. The finding isn't hard; they have a very distinctive odor. The picking sometimes is because the bushes are sometimes high (thus the name) and always hard to get at.

Pick some underripe berries (lighter in colour) as well as fully ripe ones.

Wash and place in a large saucepan or preserving kettle. Add just enough water to be visible through the fruit. Bring to a boil and simmer until soft.

Strain through a jelly bag overnight.

Measure the juice and for each cup of juice, stir in 1 cup sugar (250 mL). Bring to a boil and boil uncovered for 10 minutes or until jelly begins to form. Check by cooling a bit on a spoon. If it begins to hold a shape, the jelling has begun. If you're using a jelly thermometer, the fruit and sugar should register about 220°F (110°C). Skim off the foam as the mixture cooks.

Ladle into sterilized jars and seal while hot with a thin layer of melted paraffin.

The same method can be used for other fruits with a high pectin content . . . as with crabapples, for instance.

BEET JELLY

6 or 7 beets, cooked to make
  6 cups beet juice
juice of 2 lemons
2 pkgs. (2 oz. each) certo
8 cups sugar
2 pkgs. (3 oz. each) grape jelly powder

6 or 7 beets, tooked to make
  1.5 L beet juice
juice of 2 lemons
2 pkgs. (57 g each) certo
2 L sugar
2 pkgs. (85 g each) grape jelly powder

Wash, peel and dice the beets, cover with at least 8 cups (2L) water and cook until tender. Drain but be careful to reserve the juice. The juice is what's used in this recipe. The cooked beets can be used for supper.

Boil the 6 cups (1.5 L) beet juice with lemon juice and certo for 5 minutes. Add sugar and boil another 10 minutes. Remove from heat and stir in jelly powder.

Pour into hot sterilized jelly jars.

SPICED CRABAPPLE JELLY

crabapples	crabapples
water	water
lemon juice	lemon juice
cinnamon	cinnamon
sugar	sugar

Wash and quarter as many crabapples as you wish to use. Put them in a heavy enamel or stainless steel pan and add water just until you see it through the top layer of fruit. Do not add so much the fruit is floating. The idea is to extract the juice of the fruit, not make jelly from a watered down mixture.

Cover and cook for about ½ hour or until the fruit is soft. Mash and stir the mixture occasionally as it cooks.

Wet the jelly bag and wring it out. Then pour in the crabapple mixture. Hang the bag to drain over a bowl if the bag is strong enough; otherwise let the bag drain into a colander. For clear jelly, don't squeeze the bag. Squeezing tends to muddy the juice. Let drain for several hours or overnight.

Now, measure the strained juice and put it into the large enamel or stainless steel pan again. For every cup (250 mL) of juice, add 1 tbsp. (15 mL) lemon juice and a pinch of cinnamon. Simmer the juice for about 5 minutes, skimming off any froth that forms.

While the juice is simmering, measure out ⅔ cup (150 mL) sugar for every cup (250 mL) of fruit juice. Put it in a metal bowl or baking pan and heat it thoroughly in the oven. Add to the simmering juice and stir carefully until the sugar is dissolved. Keep at a simmer. Cook until the jelly stage is reached — a time that can vary from 10 minutes to 30 minutes. However, test as you go along. Take a bit of the simmering mixture on a spoon and cool it quickly. If the mixture jells, you have probably cooked it long enough. Also, if the bit on the spoon gathers and falls in a single large drop, then the jelly stage is complete.

The jelly stage is reached more quickly with tart fruits like crabapples. Test in this case after 10 minutes and expect it to be ready by 20 . . , unless the crabapples were older and more mellow. Then they might require the half hour.

Pour into sterilized glasses and cover with melted paraffin immediately.

CRANBERRY SAUCE

1 large orange, pulp & rind	1 large orange, pulp & rind
4 cups raw cranberries	1 L raw cranberries
2 cups sugar	500 mL sugar

Grind (or use food processor) the orange and cranberries. Add sugar and let stand for a couple of hours. Freeze in small containers.

Delicious with chicken and turkey.

SPICY RHUBARB JAM

6 cups prepared rhubarb	1.5 L prepared rhubarb
1 cup water	250 mL water
1 tbsp. preserved ginger, cut fine	15 mL preserved ginger cut fine
1 cup raisins	250 mL raisins
½ cup almonds, finely chopped	125 mL almonds, finely chopped
1 tsp. grated lemon rind	5 mL grated lemon rind
1 tsp. grated orange rind	5 mL grated orange rind
5 cups sugar	1.25 L sugar
1 cup brown sugar	250 mL brown sugar
1 box powdered fruit pectin	57 g powdered fruit pectin

Wash the rhubarb and cut into ½" (1 cm) lengths. Put it into a large heavy saucepan along with the water, ginger, raisins, almonds, lemon rind and orange rind.

Measure out the sugars and set aside.

Add the powdered fruit pectin to the rhubarb mixture and mix well. Place over high heat and stir continually until the mixture comes to a hard boil. Immediately stir in the sugars and return to a rolling boil. Cook and stir for another two minutes.

Remove from the heat and skim off the foam with a metal spoon. Stir and skim, for another five minutes or so to cool the mixture and to prevent floating fruit.

Ladle quickly into sterilized glasses and cover at once with ⅛" (8 mm) of hot paraffin.

Yields about 10 medium glasses.

GOOSEBERRY MARMALADE

gooseberries	gooseberries
sugar	sugar
water	water

Wash and pick over the gooseberries, removing stems and tails. Put them into a large heavy saucepan. For every quart of berries (4 cups or 1 L), add one cup of water. Cook slowly until the berries are soft. Measure the pulp.

For every cup of pulp, add one cup (250 mL) of sugar to the mixture. Return to the stove. Boil slowly once again until the marmalade is thick. It may take up to 20 minutes. Stir continually to prevent the mixture from sticking.

Pour into hot sterilized jars and seal.

RHUBARB CHUTNEY

10 cups rhubarb chunks	2.5 L rhubarb chunks
7 cups sugar	1.75 L sugar
2 cups cider vinegar	500 mL cider vinegar
2 tsp. cinnamon	10 mL cinnamon
2 tsp. allspice	10 mL allspice
1 tsp. cloves	5 mL cloves

Combine all the ingredients in a large heavy saucepan. Bring to a boil and let simmer, uncovered, for about 1-1½ hours. Stir occasionally to prevent sticking.

When the relish is thick and shiny, pour into hot sterilized jars and seal.

Good with cold meats — cold roast, ham or chicken.

DILL PICKLES

13 cups water	3.25 L water
1 scant cup salt	scant 250 mL salt
1 cup vinegar	250 mL vinegar
cucumbers	cucumbers
fresh dill	fresh dill

Clean and pack cucumbers into hot sterile jars. Put a piece of fresh dill in the bottom and top of each jar.

Boil together the water, salt and vinegar for 3 minutes and then pour immediately over the packed cucumbers. Seal.

Put newspapers under the sealers in storage as liquid sometimes works out as the cukes dill.

DILL PICKLES

6 lbs. cucumbers	3 kg cucumbers
dill	dill
garlic	garlic
alum*	alum*
cream of tartar	cream of tartar
2 quarts water	2 L water
1 quart vinegar	1 L vinegar
½ cup pickling salt	125 mL pickling salt

Into sterilized jars place a piece of dill in bottom plus a clove of garlic. Fill with washed cucumbers. Put a piece of dill on top and add to each quart a bit of alum and a bit of cream of tartar (each the size of a pea).

Bring the water, vinegar and pickling salt to a boil and pour into jars while hot. Seal. This recipe makes about 6 quarts. Store for at least six weeks before using.

*Alum can be found in the spice section of grocery stores or in a drugstore.

DILL PICKLES, ONCE AGAIN WITH FEELING

10 lbs. cucumbers, 2-4" long	5 kg cucumbers, 5-10 cm long
fresh dill	fresh dill
garlic cloves (optional)	garlic cloves (optional)
1 gallon water	4 L water
1 cup pickling salt	250 mL pickling salt
4 cups white vinegar	1 L white vinegar

Scrub fresh cucumbers and let soak in cold water overnight.

In the morning, pack drained cucumbers into sterilized jars. Add generous amounts of fresh dill and one clove of garlic, if desired, to each jar.

Boil water, salt and vinegar until all the salt is dissolved. Pour the hot brine over the cold cucumbers and seal. Let sit for six weeks to three months before using.

Makes approximately 10 quarts.

DILLED CARROTS

4 quarts fresh small carrots	4 L fresh small carrots
fresh dill	fresh dill
½ cup table salt	125 mL table salt
2 cups white vinegar	500 mL white vinegar
6 cups water	1.5 L water

Place carrots in sterilized quart sealers with a generous piece of fresh dill. Bring the remaining ingredients to a boil. Pour hot liquid over carrots. Seal. Let stand in a cool place for at least 6 weeks.

BEET PICKLES

12 cups prepared beets	3 L prepared beets
2 cups vinegar	500 mL vinegar
2 cups sugar	500 mL sugar
2 cups water	500 mL water
1 tsp. allspice	5 mL allspice
1 tsp. cinnamon	5 mL cinnamon
1 tbsp. whole cloves	15 mL whole cloves
(tied in cheesecloth)	(tied in cheesecloth)

Prepare beets. Select small young 1½-2" (4-5 cm) beets. Scrub and leave root and 1-2" (2.5-5 cm) of stem on. Cook until just tender. Dip in cold water and remove skins. Leave whole; slice or quarter larger beets.

Combine remaining ingredients in saucepan. Bring to a boil and boil 5 minutes. Remove spice bag. Pack hot, sterilized jars with beets. Pour hot syrup over beets to completely cover them. Seal. Yields 6 pints (3 L).

ONION AND CUCUMBER RELISH

7 cucumbers, fairly large*	7 cucumbers, fairly large*
5 large onions	5 large onions
¼ cup salt	50 mL salt
2 cups cider vinegar	500 mL cider vinegar
1 cup water	250 mL water
3½ cups sugar	875 mL sugar
½ cup flour	125 mL flour
4 tbsp. dry mustard	50 mL dry mustard
1 tsp. turmeric	5 mL turmeric

Cut cucumbers and onions quite fine. Sprinkle lightly with salt. Let stand 2 hours and drain. Rinse with cold water and drain again.

In a large saucepan, combine the vinegar, water, sugar, flour and dry mustard. Stir thoroughly to remove any lumps and cook until thickened. Then add vegetables and cook together for about 20 minutes, or until thick and clear. Add turmeric; stir well and pour into hot sterile jars. Seal.

*You can use half and half cucumbers and zucchini. If you have a food processor, it works well for cutting up these vegetables.

PICKLED ZUCCHINI

2 lbs. small zucchini (about 4 cups)	1 L small zucchini
2 medium onions	2 medium onions
¼ cup coarse salt	50 mL coarse salt
2 cups vinegar	500 mL vinegar
1 cup sugar	250 mL sugar
2 tsp. mustard seed	10 mL mustard seed
1 tsp. celery seed	5 mL celery seed
1 tsp. turmeric	5 mL turmeric

Cut zucchini and onions in very thin slices. Add salt and cover with ice water. Let stand 2 hours and drain.

In large saucepan combine remaining ingredients and bring to a boil. Add zucchini and onions. Return to heat and boil for two minutes. Pack in hot sterilized jars and seal.

Most homemakers could make sauerkraut in the early days. It was a reliable — albeit tedious — means of preserving a vegetable for the winter months.

Mom was never too comfortable with her crocks of sauerkraut. I can remember peeking into a crock to see if it was doing what it should, and then piling a heavy rock back on top of the crock for some reason or other. We always had a rock holding down a plate holding down the sauerkraut. Maybe it was feared the whole thing would escape somehow!

But others made sauerkraut without batting an eye or piling a rock.

Sister-in-law Margie makes hers in quart jars now, no more messy steaming crocks. She just makes up as many jars as is convenient at the time, instead of having to slice cabbage for days on end.

She got the recipe from Mrs. Banks who taught Dad how to cook when he arrived in the country in the late twenties and is still available to teach the second and third generations!

Incidentally, Margie says the cabbage in the jars can be used for coleslaw until it finally krauts in 3-6 weeks time.

SAUERKRAUT MADE IN JARS

Shred cabbage and pack in sterile quart jars. Add 1 tsp. (5 mL) salt, 2 tbsp. (25 mL) vinegar to each jar. Pour boiling water over kraut in jars and seal.

Set on lower shelf as it may run over as it krauts; this will not hurt it. See that water is up to neck of jar, no further. Pack cabbage hard. Let set 5 or 6 weeks before using.

FREEZER TOMATO SAUCE

20 large tomatoes, washed & cored	20 large tomatoes, washed & cored
4 large onions	4 large onions
4 large carrots	4 large carrots
½ cup chopped parsley	125 mL chopped parsley
3 tbsp. sugar	50 mL sugar
2 tbsp. salt	30 mL salt
¾ tsp. pepper	3 mL pepper

Chop the vegetables and bring to boil slowly in large pot, stirring often. Add the sugar and seasonings. Simmer 30 minutes. Cool slightly.

Measure 3 cups (750 mL) into blender or food processor. Whirl until smooth (or leave chunky if you like). Pour into freezer containers leaving ½" (1.5 cm) head-space. Makes 11-12 cups.

SWISS CHARD RELISH

5 qts. of chard stems (20 cups)	5 L chard stems
salt	salt
7 medium onions	7 medium onions
1 quart vinegar	1 L vinegar
4 cups sugar	1 L sugar
1 tbsp. celery seed	15 mL celery seed
1 tbsp. mustard seed	15 mL mustard seed
½ cup cornstarch	125 mL cornstarch
1 tsp. turmeric	5 mL turmeric
1 tsp. curry powder	5 mL curry powder
2 tbsp. dry mustard	30 mL dry mustard
½ cup cold water	125 mL cold water

Cut chard stems into small pieces and sprinkle with salt. Include a bit of the green for color. Cover with ice water and let stand for 2 hours.

Cut up the onions and add to chard. Let stand another half hour and then drain well. Cover with vinegar, sugar, celery seed and mustard seed. Put into a heavy pot and cook until tender.

In a small bowl, make a sauce of the cornstarch, turmeric, curry powder, dry mustard and cold water. Add to the hot chard mixture. Boil vigorously for 15 minutes.

Pour into sterilized jars.

Makes approximately 12 pints.

RHUBARB RELISH

4 cups rhubarb, chopped	1 L rhubarb, chopped
2 cups brown sugar	500 mL brown sugar
1 tsp. salt	5 mL salt
1 tsp. cloves	5 mL cloves
1 tsp. ginger	5 mL ginger
2 cups onions, chopped fine	500 mL onions, chopped fine
2 cups vinegar	500 mL vinegar
1 tsp. cinnamon	5 mL cinnamon
1 tsp. allspice	5 mL allspice

Chop the rhubarb into 1" (3 cm) pieces and cover with brown sugar. Let stand for a few hours or overnight until the juice comes out of the fruit.

Add the other ingredients and cook in a heavy pan until the rhubarb is tender and the mixture is thick and shiny.

Pour into sterilized jars and seal.

BEET RELISH

4 cups cooked beets, chopped	1 L cooked beets, chopped
4 cups raw cabbage, chopped	1 L raw cabbage, chopped
½ cup grated horseradish	125 mL grated horseradish
2 tsp. salt	10 mL salt
dash of pepper	dash of pepper
2 cups white vinegar	500 mL white vinegar
1½ cups sugar	375 mL sugar

Cook the beets, peel and put through a food grinder or processor to make 4 cups (1 L). Chop the cabbage in like manner. If you are using fresh horseradish, chop it also. Combine the three chopped vegetables in a large heavy pan. Season with salt and pepper.

Heat the vinegar in another pan and add the sugar, stirring carefully to completely dissolve the sugar. Add to the vegetable mixture.

Cook over low heat until all vegetables are tender — about 10 or 15 minutes. Pour into hot sterilized jars and seal.

Makes about 5 pints.

THOUSAND ISLAND RELISH

8 large cucumbers	8 large cucumbers
2-3 heads cauliflower	2-3 heads cauliflower
1 head cabbage (small)	1 head cabbage (small)
6 onions	6 onions
4 green peppers	4 green peppers
Optional: zucchini and green tomato	Optional: zucchini and green tomato
¾ cup coarse salt	175 mL coarse salt
5 cups water	1.25 L water
2 cups cold water	500 mL cold water
6 cups sugar	1.5 L sugar
¾ cup flour	175 mL flour
6 tbsp. dry mustard	75 mL dry mustard
1 tbsp. turmeric	15 mL turmeric
1 tbsp. celery seed	15 mL celery seed
1 tbsp. mustard seed	15 mL mustard seed
6 cups vinegar	1.5 L vinegar

Grind vegetables or use a food processor. Drain and cover with the coarse salt and 5 cups (1.25 L) water. Let stand at least one hour. Drain well.

Use cold water to make a paste of sugar, flour and spices. Add vinegar and cook until thick. Add the sauce to vegetables and cook for 20 minutes. Pour into sterilized jars and seal.

AUTUMN RELISH

2 cups chopped cabbage	500 mL chopped cabbage
1 cup green pepper, chopped	250 mL green pepper, chopped
1 cup sweet red pepper, chopped	250 mL sweet red pepper, chopped
4 cups cucumber, chopped	1 L cucumbers, chopped
2 cups onions, chopped	500 mL onions, chopped
4 cups ripe tomatoes, chopped	1 L ripe tomatoes, chopped
½ cup pickling salt	125 mL pickling salt
4 cups sugar	1 L sugar
2 tsp. dry mustard	10 mL dry mustard
¼ tsp. turmeric	1 mL turmeric
1 tsp. paprika	5 mL paprika
2 cups vinegar	500 mL vinegar
3 cups water	750 mL water

Chop the vegetables. Put them into a large crock or enamel container and sprinkle well with salt. Let stand overnight. The next morning, drain well, pressing out all the liquid.

Place in a large kettle and add the remaining ingredients. Cook over medium heat for 1 hour or until thick and clear. Stir occasionally. Pour into hot sterile jars and seal.

VI'S ANTIPASTO

2 cans pimento (4 oz. each)	2 cans pimento (114 g each)
2 large green peppers	2 large green peppers
4 tbsp. olive oil	50 mL olive oil
2 cans mushrooms (10 oz. each)	2 cans mushrooms (284 mL each)
2 cups sweet pickle relish *	500 mL sweet pickle relish *
4 cloves garlic, minced	4 cloves garlic, minced
½ tsp. cinnamon	2 mL cinnamon
2 bay leaves, crumbled	2 bay leaves, crumbled
1 cup cider vinegar	250 mL cider vinegar
2 jars chili sauce (15 oz. each)	2 jars chili sauce (426 g each)
2 bottles ketchup (15 oz. each)	2 bottles ketchup (426 g each)
2 doz. green olives, sliced	2 doz. green olives, sliced
2 doz. black pitted olives, sliced	2 doz. black pitted olives, sliced
2 tins solid tuna with oil (7 oz. each)	2 tins solid tuna with oil (220 g each)

Grind the pimento and green pepper in a food chopper or processor. In a large heavy pot or Dutch oven, fry the pimento and green pepper in hot olive oil. When partially cooked, add drained mushrooms, pickle relish, garlic, cinnamon and bayleaf. Once that mixture has heated to the boiling point, add the vinegar. Bring to boiling again and add ketchup and chili sauce. Boil again. Add olives and tuna. (Leave the oil on the tuna) Simmer the whole concoction for 10 minutes and then remove from heat.

When cool, put in sterilized jars or plastic containers and freeze. It will keep in the refrigerator for several months, and in the freezer for much longer.

*The green pickle relish, not the mustard variety.

MUSTARD PICKLES

1 large cauliflower	1 large cauliflower
¼ cup salt	50 mL salt
7-8 large cucumbers, cut fine	7-8 large cucumbers, cut fine
12 small cucumbers, left whole	12 small cucumbers, left whole
12 large onions, cut fine	12 large onions, cut fine
3 cups small silverskin onions	750 mL small silverskin onions
1 bunch celery, cut fine	1 bunch celery, cut fine
3 red peppers, cut fine	3 red peppers, cut fine
¾ cup pickling salt	175 mL pickling salt
5 cups white sugar	1.25 L white sugar
1 quart (4 cups) white vinegar	1 L white vinegar
2 tbsp. white mustard seed	30 mL white mustard seed
2 tbsp. celery seed	30 mL celery seed
¾ cup flour	175 mL flour
¼ cup dry mustard	50 mL dry mustard
1 tbsp. turmeric	15 mL turmeric
1½ cups vinegar or water	375 mL vinegar or water

Break the cauliflower into flowerettes; cover with boiling water. Sprinkle with ¼ cup (50 mL) salt and let stand overnight.

Cut up the rest of the vegetables and put into another large pan. Cover with boiling water. Sprinkle with the remaining ¾ cup (175 mL) salt and let stand overnight.

The next morning, drain both sets of vegetables well, rinse in cold water and drain again. Put all the vegetables into one large heavy pot.

In a smaller pot, mix together the sugar, vinegar, mustard seed, celery seed. Bring to a boil and pour over the vegetables. Now bring the vegetables to a boil.

In the meantime, mix the flour, dry mustard and turmeric. Before adding any liquid to these dry ingredients, taste the vegetable mixture to see if it's as sour and tangy as you like. If it is, use 1½ cups (375 mL) water instead of the vinegar. If the vegetables could stand to be a bit stronger, use vinegar. Make sure the flour is completely mixed into the liquid. Add a bit of the hot liquid to the mustard mixture and then put all of the mustard into the main pot. Cook until thick and smooth. The time depends on the size of the chopped vegetables, but it shouldn't be too long. You want the vegetables crisp. Pour into hot sterilized jars and seal immediately.

The Peace River country was a bit of a shock to the young bride from Europe.

In describing this new country, her husband had edited his letters carefully. As she said later, "He told me the truth, only there was so much truth he hadn't thought to tell. A man sees things differently."

You've had glimpses here and there of "the way we were" and "the food we ate" as we grew up on our farm in the Peace River country.

Perhaps you're curious about the end of this particular story. In other words, did we all live happily ever after?

More or less.

The second generation is a healthy bunch for which we have to give some credit to the wholesome and balanced diet we enjoyed. Also to the self reliance we had to develop, necessity being the mother of growth.

Our folks are not always so well, however, what with various problems caused by hard work and old age.

The farm is suffering drought this year. If it isn't one thing, it's another in this business of farming. Jim had to plow under some of his crop last week and it hurt to watch. Land is not intended to be idle and unproductive.

But there are problems in many other businesses as well. Times are tough all over, and it's hard to know where to turn.

When Nellie McClung, the great Western Canadian feminist, author and politician, lost her provincial riding by a mere 60 votes, she was seized with a desire to cook.

"I'm ashamed to have to tell it but I got more comfort that day out of my cooking spree than I did from either my philosophy or my religion . . . . I do not think I could have endured it if my cooking had gone wrong, but nothing failed me and no woman can turn out an oven full of good flaky pies with well-cooked undercrusts and not find peace for her troubled soul."*

So it's Home on the Range time again, time to cook up a storm and gather the family around the kitchen table. The important things of life have a way of surfacing in the kitchen, as we prepare and share our daily bread.

We hope our book helps in more ways than one!

Read, eat and enjoy.

*From "The Stream Runs Fast" by Nellie L. McClung. Thomas Allen, 1945.

INDEX

A Great
Gift Idea

*For Family
and Friends*

— **who enjoy good
food**

— **who enjoy
reminiscing
about the
good (and
bad) old
days**

— **who want
thrifty,
tasty meals**

Please send _____ copies of *"Home on the Range"* at *$12.95 per copy plus $2.00 per order for handling and shipping.*

NAME _____

STREET _____

CITY _____

PROVINCE _____ POSTAL CODE _____

Make cheque or money order payable to **Deadwood Publishing Ltd.** and mail to P.O. Box 564, Station G, Calgary, Alberta T3A 2G4.

(Prices subject to change without notice)

Please send _____ copies of *"Home on the Range"* at *$12.95 per copy plus $2.00 per order for handling and shipping.*

NAME _____

STREET _____

CITY _____

PROVINCE _____ POSTAL CODE _____

Make cheque or money order payable to **Deadwood Publishing Ltd.** and mail to P.O. Box 564, Station G, Calgary, Alberta T3A 2G4.

(Prices subject to change without notice)

Please send _____ copies of *"Home on the Range"* at *$12.95 per copy plus $2.00 per order for handling and shipping.*

NAME _____

STREET _____

CITY _____

PROVINCE _____ POSTAL CODE _____

Make cheque or money order payable to **Deadwood Publishing Ltd.** and mail to P.O. Box 564, Station G, Calgary, Alberta T3A 2G4.

(Prices subject to change without notice)

A Great
Gift Idea

*For Family
and Friends*

— **who enjoy good
food**

— **who enjoy
reminiscing
about the
good (and
bad) old
days**

— **who want
thrifty,
tasty meals**

Please send _____ copies of *"Home on the Range"* at $12.95 per copy plus $2.00 per order for handling and shipping.

NAME_____

STREET_____

CITY_____

PROVINCE _____ POSTAL CODE _____

Make cheque or money order payable to **Deadwood Publishing Ltd.** and mail to P.O. Box 564, Station G, Calgary, Alberta T3A 2G4.

(Prices subject to change without notice)

Please send _____ copies of *"Home on the Range"* at $12.95 per copy plus $2.00 per order for handling and shipping.

NAME_____

STREET_____

CITY_____

PROVINCE _____ POSTAL CODE _____

Make cheque or money order payable to **Deadwood Publishing Ltd.** and mail to P.O. Box 564, Station G, Calgary, Alberta T3A 2G4.

(Prices subject to change without notice)

Please send _____ copies of *"Home on the Range"* at $12.95 per copy plus $2.00 per order for handling and shipping.

NAME_____

STREET_____

CITY_____

PROVINCE _____ POSTAL CODE _____

Make cheque or money order payable to **Deadwood Publishing Ltd.** and mail to P.O. Box 564, Station G, Calgary, Alberta T3A 2G4.

(Prices subject to change without notice)